FOCUS LESSONS

FOCUS LESSONS

How Photography Enhances the Teaching of Writing

RALPH FLETCHER

HEINEMANN
Portsmouth, NH

Heinemann
361 Hanover Street
Portsmouth, NH 03801–3912
www.heinemann.com

Offices and agents throughout the world

The author and publisher wish to thank those who have generously given permission to reprint borrowed material:

"The Self-E Expression Project with Joan McGarry" by Joan McGarry. Copyright © the Westmoreland Museum of American Art. Reprinted by permission of the Westmoreland Museum of American Art.

Image Credits
Page 78: John Filo/Getty Images
Page 83: Bill Owens/Suburbia
Page 96: Courtesy of Tim Reisert
Page 99: Courtesy of Jen Greene
Remainder of photographs copyright © Ralph Fletcher

ISBN: 978-0-325-10917-6
Library of Congress Control Number: 2019943393

Editor: Holly Kim Price
Production: Victoria Merecki
Cover and interior designs: Monica Ann Crigler
Typesetter: Gina Poirier Design
Manufacturing: Steve Bernier

Printed in the United States of America on acid-free paper
23 22 21 20 19 VP 1 2 3 4 5

This one is for M.M.

CONTENTS

How to Access Online Resources

All of the photos in this book are available online. To access them go to:

http://hein.pub/focuslessons-login

Log in with your username and password. If you do not already have an account with Heinemann, you will need to create an account.

On the Welcome page, choose "Click here to register an Online Resource."

Register your product by entering the code: RFPHOTO (be sure to read and check the acknowledgment box under the keycode).

Once you have registered your product, it will appear alphabetically in your account list of My Online Resources.

Note: When returning to Heinemann.com to access your previously registered products, simply log into your Heinemann account and click on "View my registered Online Resources."

[◎] ACKNOWLEDGMENTS

"Ralph Fletcher has a new book." That sentence makes it sound like it's my work, and mine alone, a solitary endeavor. In fact, a professional book is much more of a joint effort than you might imagine. That's especially true when an author ventures into unfamiliar territory, as I did in writing *Focus Lessons*.

My thinking about the connections between photography and writing (and teaching) evolved through dialogue with many teachers including Abby Brewer, Nancy Costanzo, Dylan Crettol, Teri Rucinsky, Jodi O'Rourke, Megan Mordan, Rebekah O'Dell, Erika Victor, Leonor Jimenez-Ethier, Martie Hoofer, Valerie Golden, Jennifer Sniadecki, Heather Lambright, Kimberelle Martin, Abbie Wence, Alana Van Der Slurs, Debbie Goldsworthy, Trish Walton, Melissa Wood-Glusac, Anna Rekate, Debbie Robl, Judy Nadler, Andrea Smith, Danielle Vaccaro, Melanie Spence, Erin McCoy. I am especially grateful to Adam Myman, Janelle Barker, Tim Reisert, and Jen Greene. Thanks to Valerie Piccini and Darren Victory.

Thanks to my colleagues Carl Anderson, Valerie Bang-Jensen, Trevor Bryan, Chris Crutcher, Dan Feigelson, Lester Laminack, Barry Lane, Mark Lubkowitz, Frank Serafini, Stacey Shubitz, Franki Sibberson, and Annie Ward.

I appreciate the students whose work is included here, especially Eric Verrico-Choi, an eighth grader. I'm grateful to Dana Johansen, a teacher who helped me gather student work. Thanks to Aaron, Solomon, Jess, and JoAnn for making the photos sparkle. Thanks, Spaz—you are a true original.

Thanks to Michael Gonchar and Yoon Kang-O'Higgins.

I have been learning from a number of professional photographers who are also wonderful teachers: Artie Morris, Glenn Bartley, David H. Wells, Alan Murphy, Greg Basco, Juan Pons, and Sarah Skinner. Frank Serafini has been a mentor in this regard. Other photographers provided insights that are included in the book: Joshua Cripps, David Pritchett, Dustin Sparks, Guy Tal, William Allard, Annie McKinnell, and Spencer Cox.

I am particularly grateful to photographer Wendy Ewald, who was generous with her time. Thanks to Joan McGarry. I can't say enough about Marvin Heiferman, a smart thinker and influential figure in the world of photography. Marvin was a terrific sounding board, and connected me to several important books and photographers.

Tom Newkirk and I kicked around this topic over breakfast at Sunny's Restaurant one morning. A talk with Tom Newkirk is always helpful in getting my creative juices flowing and helping me envision what direction a new project might take.

I'm grateful for several conversations I had with the late, great Paul Janeczko.

Thanks to my buddy Mike McCormick.

My wife, JoAnn, ventured into the visual world long before I did. I have had umpteen conversations with her about art, painting, composition. . . . These talks have helped me develop whatever aesthetic I have. JoAnn has been a steady source of support and encouragement—always.

A highly visual book like this represents a new direction for Heinemann. I wondered what speed bumps we might encounter along the way, but I must say that the Heinemann team—including Josh Evans, Krysten Lebel, and Victoria Merecki—has been fantastic. My editor, Holly Price, had an early, important influence on this book and was a steadfast support in helping me to shape it along the way. I couldn't have written it without you, Holly.

Introduction

First, let's get the jokes out of the way.

It's early spring and I'm crouched at the edge of a pond, photographing hooded mergansers, or trying to anyway. I've got my gear ready: tripod, camera mounted with my longest telephoto lens (the one my sons refer to as my *obnoxious* lens). The jumbo lens definitely draws attention to itself. A young couple comes strolling by. The guy catches my eye and grins.

"Think that lens is big enough?"

He giggles at his original wit; in fact, I've heard that one a few hundred times before. Wisecracks about lens size seem to come with the territory. Believe it or not, the lens is probably *not* big enough for what I'm trying to do. The mergansers are beautiful but skittish; they stubbornly keep their distance. When you're shooting wildlife you almost never have enough "reach" to pull the animal in as close as you'd like. But I play along, offering a shrug along with an easy, what-are-you-gonna-do smile.

Later that day a friend remarks: "Hey, Ralph, I saw those pictures you posted on Facebook. Wow, your camera takes great pictures!"

I've heard that one before, too, but this time I'm ready.

"Yes," I say, quickly adding: "And my laptop writes great stories!"

I consider this an extremely clever comeback, though it's possible I'm the only one who does. My friend gives me a puzzled smile.

"Um, yeah, well . . . Anyway I wanted to ask, what kind of equipment do you use?"

"My eyes," I tell him.

— ✳ —

I take photographs every chance I get. I suppose that makes me a photographer. It's a relatively new field to me, so I really don't have a deep knowledge of its history. I knew the big names, of course—Diane Arbus, Ansel Adams, Alfred Stieglitz, the controversial Robert Mapplethorpe—but that's about it. Turns out a Frenchman named Joseph Nicehore Niépce took the first photograph back in 1826. In the United States the Civil War was the first armed conflict documented by photographers (Matthew Brady, Alexander Gardner, and Timothy O'Sullivan).

Those early photographers were pioneers, oddball loners who lugged cumbersome equipment from place to place. Ansel Adams carried a box camera into the mountains when he created his iconic black-and-white landscapes. Gradually, aided by technological advances, photography began to change. Cameras got better, smaller, and more affordable. Kodak released the Brownie camera in 1900. Edward Land introduced the Polaroid instant camera in 1948.

Since then photography has exploded. The art of photography (the word means *drawing with light*) was once considered a rarified activity practiced by a select few experts; suddenly it became available to everybody. In 2015 it was estimated people were taking more pictures in two minutes than had ever existed 150 years ago. (Note: This deluge of images has hurt professional photographers. Fifteen or twenty years ago you could make decent money selling your photos to stock photo companies, but that's no longer true. Today the supply of visual images is so plentiful the market for stock photos has largely dried up.)

The invention of the digital camera democratized photography. No more film. No more darkroom with pans of smelly chemical soaks. No more paying to have your rolls of film developed and printed.

Think about it: at age ten or twelve most kids in this country get a cell phone. Smartphones come equipped with a sophisticated camera. It's practically a rite of passage. The photographs we take are supremely important to us. They record our "Kodak moments," small and large. They function as our

memory banks, often supplanting what actually happened. When it's time to get a new cell phone, we nervously ask the guy at the Verizon store: "Are you sure you can transfer all my pictures to my new phone?"

Although such historical context is important, I hope it doesn't sound as if I'm trying to ride the latest fad, like crowdfunding. This book is rooted in my journey into photography, which has been an intensely personal one. I have always had a deep curiosity about the natural world: spiders, dolphins, elephants, raptors. When I started taking photos, it felt like a door into the natural world swung open. No longer was I limited to seeing exotic creatures on Animal Planet or in the pages of *National Geographic*. Now I could observe them through the lens of my camera. Capturing those images allowed me to savor and study as I "reread" them again and again.

I participated in a trip to Costa Rica led by professional photographers Glenn Bartley and Greg Basco. We took pictures of toucans, tanagers, motmots, and so many dazzling hummingbirds I could scarcely keep track of them. One night we ventured into the rain forest in search of the Pallas' long-tongued bat. We stood for over an hour in pitch darkness. Later that night, looking through the viewfinder of my camera, I reviewed my images.

Look at those wings! That face! That pink tongue! I was astonished to see *that* image in *my* camera. Of course, I can't take all the credit. Mother Nature created the exotic bat. Our trip leaders found the location and suggested the proper settings. Nevertheless, I took the picture. A photo like that went a long way toward fueling my confidence. It wasn't just a pipe dream—that picture provided indisputable proof that I could become a strong photographer. And I knew I would continue to improve if I invested the necessary time and persistence.

Most people know me as a writer. I've written and cowritten books on the craft of writing. I believe that writing is not simply a matter of inspiration, genius, or inborn talent. There are particular ways in which words, sentences, and paragraphs work together to create the effect you want.

In this book I will explore the interplay between photography and writing. I will straddle those two worlds and ferry between them. This book is based on two basic ideas:

*Photography is important in and of itself. We may tend to think of photography as a fringe subject, a creative elective taken by high school students, but it's much more than that. Like it or not, the world is becoming increasingly visual. The students in our classrooms write the stories of their lives (trips, triumphs, disasters, loves, celebrations) via the photos they take every day with their smartphones. This is a sea change in our culture—we ignore it at our peril. It behooves us to deepen our knowledge of photography.

*There are strong links between photography and writing. This is true in substance and process, as well as language. The world of photography provides a visual, concrete language (angle, focus, point of view, close-up, panorama) that is enormously helpful in teaching writing. Lo and behold, we may discover that students are already familiar with this terminology. It makes sense for teachers to bring this visual language into the writing classroom.

Moreover, we'll find that there's a great deal of overlap between the craft of photography and the craft of writing. It turns out that photography can illuminate the craft of writing and help us understand it in a whole new way.

PART ONE

The Journey

Getting Close:
A Personal Note

In high school I had a close friend. Out of respect for his privacy I'll refer to him only by his first initial: M. In some ways he was like my sixth brother. We were inseparable. We knew each other's secrets. We concocted a catchphrase for our friendship: E.E.T., an acronym for Experience Everything Together. That may sound ridiculous, but back then it was a credo to live by.

M was an intense person with a wicked sense of humor. He was also a serious photographer. Twice we drove across the country in his little Datsun. Along the way he would make frequent stops to take photographs. I'd read or scribble in my notebook while he studied his light meter and set up his tripod.

"I'm losing the light!" he'd fume, standing at the edge of a wild creek in Idaho or an Iowa cornfield. M could talk photography for hours: f-stops, shutter speed, film types, ISO, depth of field, wide angle, macro, telephoto lens . . . I'd politely nod my head, half-listening, while he rambled on. Honestly, I didn't quite know what to make of the photographic world. I was amazed at all the expensive equipment, not to mention the time and energy required to keep it clean. M was extremely fastidious about this; he had various cloths for cleaning

Green-Crested Turaco

his lenses, and a can of compressed air for blowing away dust. He always ended a photo shoot by carefully cleaning each piece of equipment.

After college M and I decided to pool our talents. We began to create free-lance articles and brochures. He took the photos, I wrote the text. We even designed a snazzy business card:

Pens & Lens
We'll shoot anything that moves.

Although we didn't exactly conquer the world of photojournalism, we did have some success (several articles published in *People Magazine*). But it wasn't easy. The freelance world was brutally competitive; roughly 25,000 photographers were trying to make a living in New York City alone. After taking a hard look at his prospects, M abruptly decided to change careers. He left the world of photography, sold his equipment, and never looked back. We moved to different parts of the country but stayed in contact, visiting each other as often as possible.

Now comes the sad part of the story. My friend and I had a major falling out. He blamed me for something (an incident involving money) and abruptly ended our friendship. I've made peace with this—what choice did I have? Still, it feels like a monumental loss even now. I have other close friends, but the space M occupied in my life remains empty. Today there are many moments when I want to turn to him out of old habit to share an example of life's absurdity, something I know that only he would fully appreciate.

I haven't spoken to him in ten years.

One year my wife bought me a digital camera for Christmas. The gift surprised me. I had never hinted that I wanted a camera, because I didn't. Carefully, afraid I might drop it, I slid the camera from its box. Over the next few weeks I put aside my trepidation and began experimenting with it. I got a few nice images. Taking pictures was more fun than I expected, though I ran into challenges. Turns out that digital photography represents an unholy marriage between the computer and camera. No wonder these cameras are so complicated and their manuals so thick. I'm a poet, not an engineer! I've got a flair for creating metaphors, not absorbing technical information. But I realized I couldn't dodge the technical stuff. Sure, I could use the auto settings, but that was the lazy way out. I had to thoroughly understand the workings of my camera.

So I studied, read articles, and watched dozens of videos. I continued taking pictures. In many ways it felt like learning a new language. Slowly I achieved a halting competency, if not fluency. I signed up for an IPT (instructional photography trip) where I got to work shoulder to shoulder with a professional photographer. My photos improved. This gave me just enough inspiration to persevere and keep climbing the ladder.

I told people that photography was a new passion in my life, except that wasn't entirely true. It wasn't new, not really. It's more accurate to say that learning to take pictures has felt like rediscovering a forgotten tongue, one I'd heard spoken when I was a young man writing in my notebook while M photographed a clear Idaho stream, when we were gleefully crisscrossing the country listening to Bob Dylan and Joni Mitchell and Jackson Browne with our whole lives spread before us.

I felt a surprising ease with photography. Why? I think it's because I was lucky enough to get close to the photographic world—its peculiar language, artifacts, quirks, rhythms, joys, and frustrations—when I was a young man. I guess I was paying attention when M rambled on about photography. Some part of me must have been soaking it in. Today when I pull out my camera and get ready to shoot, it feels reconnecting with a long-lost friend.

This book is for you, M, though I know you don't need or want anything from me. Turns out it was you who inspired my love for photography, however accidentally. Talk about ironic: who could have imagined that I would end up carrying the torch you lit so many years ago?

Steep End of the Learning Curve

Fifteen years ago, my wife and coauthor JoAnn Portalupi abruptly left the field of literacy. This surprised a lot of people—I admit I didn't see it coming myself. JoAnn is a passionate learner; she hungered for a new challenge. In the years that followed she reinvented herself, becoming an accomplished fine arts painter and, most recently, a yoga instructor.

I seemed to be cut from a different cloth. Until now I've been perfectly comfortable doing what I do—teaching, speaking, and writing. Photography changed all that. I suddenly find myself on the steep end of the learning curve, trying to gain mastery over a field that is as perplexing/frustrating as it is rewarding. I've certainly learned a lot about photography, but something happened that I didn't anticipate—I've also learned a ton about writing.

My very first instructional photo trip took place on Long Island, New York, not far from where I went to high school. When I lived on Long Island before, I had no idea that Nickerson Beach and the Jamaican Bay Wildlife Refuge were rich nesting areas for birds. The photo trip was led by Arthur Morris, a professional bird photographer and former NYC teacher. I learn best by spending time with a passionate expert. Artie Morris fits the bill—he has spent forty

Key West

years photographing birds all around the world. Over the next five days he shared a range of tips and strategies for photographing wildlife. His first lesson involved sun angle, the importance of keeping the sun behind you.

"You want to shoot with the sun over your shoulder," Artie explained.

During the next four days he drilled this idea into my head. Then one morning Artie took me aside and gave me a one-to-one minilesson on back-lighting—how sunlight in front of you can be used to light the subject from behind. This surprised me—it seemed to contradict his previous instruction on sun angle—but it worked. I was pleased by the result, the skimmer chick wrapped in rosy morning light.

Later he directed me to lie down flat when I photographed another skimmer chick trying to eat a small fish one of its parents had pulled from the sea.

On that photo trip we got up each day before dawn and worked hard all morning. By 11 A.M. I was bone-tired and ready for a nap. Later the six photography students would meet for teaching sessions in Artie's hotel room.

Skimmer Chick, Backlit

"It seems that getting strong pictures depends a lot on showing up," I said to him one day. "A lot of it hinges on just being there, at the right place and time."

Artie nodded. "Yes, lots of days you get up early and shoot pictures of stuff you've seen before. Occasionally you get a picture of something you've never seen before. And once in a great while, if you're lucky, you get a picture of something nobody has ever seen before. That's special."

**Straight Bay
at First Light**

I loved this idea. And isn't writing like that, too? So much depends on butt-in-chair: sitting down at your desk. If you do that, well, anything can happen. Often you find yourself writing stuff you've written before. Occasionally you create something you've never written before. And one day, with persistence and luck, you might create something special that nobody has ever written.

I have taken several instructional photo trips and learned from each of the instructors. I try to remember those tips and skills and use them during the many hours I spend taking photos on my own. When I'm in Downeast Maine I usually get up early to catch the sunrise. I drag my camera gear down to the edge of the water. As I'm setting up my camera the words of Don Murray float into my head. "Write early, write fast."

Also, I remember something that Israeli novelist Amos Oz once said: "I write when I'm inspired . . . and I see to it that I'm inspired every morning at 9 A.M."

Show up. For wildlife photography that means showing up early. My watch says 5:45 A.M. There's no wind. A thin, ghostly mist drifts across the

Ruby-Throated Hummingbird (Female)

glassy surface of the water. The edge of this tidal river can be a promising spot. From this vantage point I have photographed raptors, shore birds, water birds, songbirds, yellow seals, and river otters. This morning there's not much wildlife stirring. Across the water there are two small islands, wrapped in shadow. I stand, waiting.

Then it happens—the first morning sunlight licks the tops of the trees on that island. I watch as the shadows on the island begin to shrink, a spectacle I've witnessed many times before, though I can't resist taking a few pictures.

Minutes later a double-crested cormorant barrels in and makes a crash-landing. It settles in a place too far away for a great photo, so I watch through my binoculars as it drifts through a patch of golden light before plunging underwater.

A loud humming startles me. Hummingbird! It's a bird you don't expect to see at the water's edge. It hovers not five feet from me, staring curiously, checking me out, before it zooms away.

Beaver

I picture JoAnn inside the house, immersed in her daily morning meditation. Photography feels like another kind a meditation. Taking pictures allows me to leave myself behind. I shed the world of words, which has been my home for many years, and immerse myself in light, shadow, and color.

Photography is akin to fishing. On many days there's nothing biting but mosquitoes and blackflies. It's no fun if you don't relish the process, the hunt. Today I can't see many birds. Maybe the wind is blowing too hard. I wonder if most birds have flown south . . . or perhaps they sense the lurking presence of an eagle.

Not that I'm complaining. Photography has introduced me to some gorgeous country, places I never would have visited otherwise. There are always flashes of beauty and daily surprises. One day I was at a pond taking pictures of nesting herons when a beaver suddenly appeared. It crawled out of the water, giving me a good look at the wide black tail. Then it slid back into the water and started swimming toward me. I watched through my camera as the

**Maine Tidal Flat
in Moonlight**

critter came closer (snap), closer (snap), closer (snap-snap) still until the thing practically crawled into my lap.

OK, so maybe a beaver isn't as exotic as an eagle, snowy owl, or humpback whale. Still, I had never gotten a point-blank look at a beaver's face. I felt thrilled and honored to share his world, to be so close to that wild creature we were practically breathing the same air.

You might object: *Well, OK, but I'm not a wildlife photographer. I don't see myself photographing beavers, eagles, or kingfishers.* Maybe not, but photographing wildlife is no different from taking pictures of a baby, a football team, or guests at a birthday party. The same principles apply. You try to get close and make yourself invisible. You try to be still enough to enter their world. You try to tell the story.

"Writing poetry puts you in a state of constant composition," Donald Graves often said. That's true for photography, as well. Taking pictures has made me more alive to my world. I'm forever on the lookout for promising images. There's a dirt road in Downeast Maine where I often pass a tidal mudflat. When the tide is out the smaller rivulets cut an organic pattern—like roots or arteries—in the mud. I have taken many photos at that spot, though nothing too exciting so far. One day I'm hoping to visit that spot under certain conditions: sunset at low tide, though not dead low. There needs to be some water in those streamlets for what I'm envisioning. I imagine a brilliant purple or pink sky reflected in those rivulets, surrounded by an expanse of mud. Now *that* could be a fabulous photo. That hasn't happened yet, at least not while I'm around, but I intend to keep coming back to that spot. As Hamlet famously said: the readiness is all.

TEACHING CONNECTIONS

I wanted to get serious about photography, and I have made some progress, but I had to push through many obstacles to do so. Most of them were more emotional than actual. I quickly discovered that being something of an expert in one realm didn't prepare me to be a rank beginner in another. The challenges I encountered are the same ones faced by our students.

Alien language. The photographic world included a perplexing new language. I encountered many strange words (*bokeh*—huh?) that stopped me cold. In addition, I came upon familiar words (*noise*) being used in peculiar new ways. At first this new lexicon felt like an impediment, reminding me at every turn of my status as a raw rookie. And yet I was determined to learn how to use these new words, partly because I knew that being able to do so would signal full membership in this club I wanted to enter.

Failure as the new norm. I lived with daily wipeout, error, and blunder. Things went wrong at least as often as they went right. I took a zillion images that were blurry or hopelessly overexposed. *Embrace failure* sounds like the kind of glib sound bite we should all accept, but can we be

continues

real for a moment? A succession of daily failure *sucks*. It hollowed me out and drained my confidence. A host of negative voices chirped nonstop in my head:

I can't do this.

I'm wasting so much time and money.

I'll never understand the technical stuff, because I'm not good at that and I never will be.

Embarrassment. The salesman at the camera store encouraged me to buy protected glass coverings for my lenses, so I dutifully forked over the dough. On the very next photo trip our instructor decided to use the lens protectors I'd purchased as a teaching point. He gathered the group and, making sure everybody could hear, loudly told me: "Here's what I want you to do, Ralph. Take these lens covers and skip them across the water, like you skim flat stones. Because they're useless . . . a total waste of money."

This encounter left me feeling stupid and naïve. I felt shame, the emotion Tom Newkirk (2017) describes so well in his book *Embarrassment*. And that wasn't the only time this happened. More than once I asked a question to an instructor who responded by giving me a look that said: *Dude, you should have figured this out by now—it's not that complicated.* Yeah, well, it was for me.

A thirst for praise. I hungered for praise—any kind word or supportive comment—and cherished it when it came. Sometimes this praise came from friends and relatives. It was even better when I received kudos from a fellow photographer. One day one of the instructors peered over my shoulder at the viewfinder on the back of my camera. I'd just taken a picture of a scarlet tanager.

continues

"Nice," he said, nodding. "I'd be thrilled with that image."

I tried to play it cool, but I couldn't pull it off. My lips twisted into a grin. A comment like that could fuel me for a long time.

Any students trying to learn a new subject could relate to the difficulties I faced. Many of us deliver instruction in a subject we have taught for years; we know it so well we could explain it in our sleep. The experience is wholly different for a student encountering a new text, task, lexicon, or subject for the first time. It's important to keep in touch with our students' experience and their status as nonexperts. Let's never forget how it feels to stand on the other side of the fence.

The Camera as Writer's Notebook

I can't remember exactly when I stopped carrying a note-book. Sometime in the past year, I gave up writing hurried descriptions of people on the subway. . . . It's not that my memory improved but, instead, that I started archiving these events and ideas with my phone, as photographs.

—Casey N. Nep, "A Thousand Words: Writing from Photographs"

Lubec, Maine. I've got my camera slung around my neck. I'm looking across a tidal river at two small, uninhabited islands a few hundred yards away. The Bay of Fundy boasts the biggest tides in the world; during certain lunar cycles they run thirty-plus feet. Now, at slack tide, the water looks calm. The early morning sun—what photographers call the *sweet light*—has morphed into something stronger. Even I know this: photographers try to

15

avoid the harsh light. My stomach growls; I start thinking about going inside for a midmorning snack.

Something sparkles on the water. At first, I'm not sure what it is . . . a small fish jumping? A closer look reveals a piece of seaweed protruding from the water, backlit by the sun and unexpectedly beautiful. I want to take a picture, but the seaweed is drifting on the current, so I have to hurry. I grab my camera but realize it's mounted with a telephoto lens, one suitable for capturing birds. Wrong lens—*argh!* To frame the seaweed properly I need to switch to my normal lens, which is what I do.

After firing off a few pictures, I pause to study them in the viewer. A few "blinkies" are flashing, which lets me know the light was brighter than I realized. I make a few adjustments, switching to a faster shutter speed and stopping down the aperture to avoid overexposing the image. I'm only able to take a few more shots before the seaweed drifts into shadow. The lovely light has vanished; still, I think I've got a few keepers.

The subject of this photo is nothing more than a lowly strand of seaweed, but that morning light transformed it into something lovely and luminous, at least to me. No doubt other interesting things had floated by that spot in the previous weeks or months, but I wasn't there to see them. To create this picture, certain elements and conditions had to be present:

- seaweed
- slack tide
- calm water
- soft, early sunlight
- someone to notice it
- available camera
- the decision to take the photograph.

Remove any one of these conditions and the photograph wouldn't exist, or would be very different. A photograph is a sacred gathering, a precise moment of time and space. Maybe that's why photos are so precious to us.

That's Mom, the summer before she died, making Toll House cookies. Look: she's wearing the pink blouse I gave her.

"Snapshots fascinate us because they are always incomplete; they demand our interaction," notes Marvin Heiferman (2012) is his book *Photography Changes Everything*. "We search them for clues, trying to remember or confirm

Floating Seaweed

who we were, who and what we've cared about, where we've been, and what we've become."

In photographing that seaweed I was using my camera very much the way I use my writer's notebook. In this chapter I'll explore ways in which my camera and writer's notebook mirror each other. The parallels are not exact. Indeed, there are important ways in which the camera and notebook differ in form, purpose, and function. But there's a remarkable deal of overlap. We may find that a camera has certain advantages over a paper notebook when it comes to fostering the creative process.

REACTING

"I'm surrounded by people who are smarter than I am," Don Murray once wrote. "They have led more interesting lives than I have. But they're not writers because they don't have the writer's habits." The first habit Murray identified? Writers react. Everybody gets ideas for a poem, book, movie, or TV show. Ideas are a dime a dozen. But a writer with an idea takes a crucial extra step—she reacts. She writes it down.

Murray's words resonate with the way I use my writer's notebook. A notebook provides the perfect place for reacting to the world. Over the years I have

Winter in Portsmouth, New Hampshire

used it as a sounding board, a place to ruminate, reflect, and react to the world. I've poured out intense feelings: sorrow, anguish, loneliness, boredom, love, and exhilaration. I've collected ideas for novels and poetry collections. If I hear a character talking in my head, I try to capture his voice by jotting the words in my notebook. My writer's notebook continues to play an invaluable part of my life as a writer and as a human being. But more and more I find myself reacting to the world via my camera—by taking photographs.

In early January I have a lunch date with author-illustrator David McPhail at RiRa's Pub in Portsmouth, New Hampshire. Afterward I head back to my car. A January thaw has turned the sidewalks from ice to slush. While walking down Market Street I happen to glance to the left. There's a short, narrow street with buildings on both sides, and a parking garage visible in the distance. I'm struck by the warm, rosy light shining on those bricks. I forgot to bring my camera—always a mistake—so I grab a few shots with my cell phone and make a mental note to come back to this spot at around 3 P.M.

Sunset from a Minivan

During the next few days the weather refuses to cooperate; there's a nasty mix of rain and snow. Then the temperatures plunge into the teens, and all that slush gets frozen. Two weeks later the temps finally jump into the high thirties. I pack camera and tripod and race into Portsmouth, only to find that the sun is hidden behind a bank of clouds. The drab light on the brick has none of the magical quality I remembered on my previous visit. I don't even bother to take my camera out of the car.

Finally, in early February, conditions look promising. The sun shines brightly as I arrive in Portsmouth at 3 P.M. In truth, the light is not *exactly* as I remembered it, but it's close enough. I'm mesmerized by the reflection in the windows, something I hadn't before noticed. I didn't remember the solitary wreath, either, which strikes me as an enduring symbol of Christmas in New England. I spend a half hour photographing.

This sequence is typical of the process I go through: notice, react, photograph. A camera gives you the perfect way to react. The speed and stealth of photography make it ideal for the fast-paced world in which we live. Look at the shadow creasing that toddler's face. Can you believe the pink light at the edge of that river? The sunset is going gangbusters outside, but that guy stays in his car absorbed in his cell phone.

BUILDING VOLUME

"What did you read when you were a kid?" asked Annie Ward, coauthor of *From Striving to Thriving* (Harvey and Ward 2017). "How did you build the necessary volume you needed to become a strong reader?"

The assumption behind this question is that a learner needs a great deal of volume, quantity, time on task to achieve proficiency. That's one of the reasons a notebook is such a great tool—a high-comfort, low-risk incubator conducive to voluminous writing that builds confidence and stamina.

"Write from abundance," Don Murray often advised. Later, the great winnowing will take place, when the writer begins to sift the wheat from the chaff. Any writer worth his salt knows that much of what you write won't be very good.

Photography follows the identical principle. To get a few strong images, you must take many bad ones. It's true that sheer quantity alone won't transform you into a skilled photographer, but without taking lots of pictures it's nearly impossible to improve your skills. Nowadays there's little downside for shooting lots of pictures—digital images are virtually free. A wedding photographer will snap several thousand photos to secure a hundred strong images that will satisfy the client. Do the same thing at your nephew's graduation. Don't hold back. Squeeze the shutter. Stay on your subject. And, as several of my photo instructors have noted, you'll certainly miss all the great shots you don't take.

COLLECTING

Crows collect sparkly things; humans are similarly inclined. The writer's notebook is a container to gather whatever you find interesting. I've found that comparing a writer's notebook to a collection strikes a chord with kids, many of whom are collectors themselves. I believe that a writer's notebook should be less text based and might include artifacts: notes, candy wrappers, fortunes from fortune cookies. Photographs are a natural addition to this list.

I'm a forager. Like many writers, I cherish the particularity of the world with all its astonishing wonder and head-shaking weirdness. I'm talking about strange little things. If I find a rock with a striking crystal or fossil, I'll tuck it in my pocket. If I come upon a hilarious misspelling on a restaurant takeout menu, I tape it into my notebook. My camera allows me to indulge this persistent itch to collect things of this world.

This suggests an important way I use my camera. It's not always about getting the perfect shot or preserving a special moment for posterity. Those are worthy endeavors, but I find that taking pictures allows me to drink in the world. I want to cast a wide net and capture objects, reflections, or shadows that strike my fancy or pique my interest. Taking a photo is my way of saying: *This may look small and random, but it matters to me. I want to bring it into my life. I don't want to forget.*

Writing off (or from) a Photograph

Photographs have certainly become important to me, but they will never replace my need for words. First and foremost, I'm a writer. Sometimes one of my photographs becomes a catalyst for writing. I often feel the impulse to add some text to the photo I've taken: adding some context, or creating a caption. In addition, I often "write off" (or from) an image. Doing so feels like riding the energy of a picture and letting it take me to a new place. I explore this idea in Chapter 8.

Play and Experimentation

I was good at goofing around when I was a kid. Today, as an adult, I'm trying to relearn this skill. My notebook has been a lifesaver in this regard. I think of my writer's notebook as a playground where ideas, projects, and language have an open field to romp and interact without any particular goal or purpose, just for the fun of it, to see what happens.

I play around when I'm taking pictures, too. I often mutter to myself: *I wonder what would happen if I try this . . . ?* Not too many years ago the high cost of film and film processing threw a wet blanket on the urge to experiment; digital photography, as already stated, changed all that. The way I experiment when taking pictures resembles the purposeful play that takes place in a writer's notebook. Often I begin with a general sense of where I want to go and improvise from there.

Case in point: I've become intrigued by the idea of creating blurs when photographing rivers and ocean waves. Some alluring images taken by other photographers inspired me to do this myself. I became a sponge and soaked up as much as I could about this subject. I read, attended several webinars, and

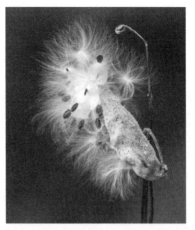

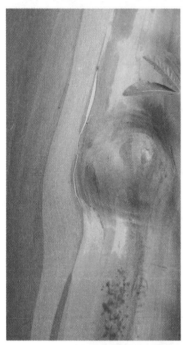

**Surf at
Hampton Beach**
watched a dozen YouTube videos from experienced photographers. Finally, I
decided to take a stab at it. I purchased a neutral density filter and screwed it
onto my lens. This filter would block out a portion of the light, allowing me to
keep the shutter open long enough to create that blurring effect. Or so I hoped.

I began experimenting. I went to the beach and tried taking images with
the shutter open for a half second, full second, three seconds, five seconds.
Slowly, through trial and error, I started to figure things out. When photographing waves I discovered that a shutter speed of five seconds yielded images with
nothing but cottony white, with very little detail on the wave itself. By using a
shorter shutter speed—a half second to a full second—I was able to produce
pleasing blurs that didn't erase all the features of the wave.

For the photo of the surf at Hampton Beach, I used a neutral density filter
that allowed me to keep the shutter open for .3 seconds. The painterly quality of
this image surprised me. I wish I could say that I knew exactly how this image
would turn out; in fact I benefited from some old-fashioned luck. I've learned
that chance features prominently whenever you experiment in photography.

"Some days you get lucky," says photographer Destin Sparks. "Other days
you wait patiently for luck to happen."

I used to feel sheepish about this, but now I accept luck as part of the deal. No, you can't rely on blind luck to fix a doomed photograph (or paragraph). But intelligent experimentation makes room for luck to sit down at your table and bring its gifts. And the camera-as-notebook is the perfect arena for fooling around and seeing what you might come up with.

My friend Artie Voigt once described the writer's notebook as a "high-comfort, low-risk place" place to write. I've always liked that description. Those same conditions are present when I've got my camera in my hand. My camera gives me another way to play with images, follow my passions, find my voice, and tell the stories I want to tell.

TEACHING CONNECTIONS

The camera-as-writer's-notebook is an emerging idea. Translation: I haven't got it all figured out. I'm hoping that educators intrigued with this idea will run with it. I believe we should think carefully about the language we use when talking about this idea to our students. Perhaps we should confer with them on their photos the same way we would confer with them on the entries in their notebook (i.e., photos = seed ideas). If you have a student who can't think of anything to write about, you might suggest: "Scroll through your photos and see if you find any pictures that pique your interest or leave you wanting to say more about it."

On the other hand . . . it might make sense to use a slightly different language, perhaps referring to students' notebooks and "photo-books" to differentiate between the two. Either way we can invite students to look through their photos and find ways to sort them. We can ask them:

Do you see any patterns?

Does anything surprise you?

What are the most powerful images, the photos you keep coming back to?

What subjects seem to draw your eye again and again?

Do any photographs make you want to write about them?

Upon Reflection

If there is magic on this planet it is contained in water.

—Loren Eiseley, *The Immense Journey*

Writers find themselves drawn to certain ideas and themes. Boxing captivated Norman Mailer. Hemingway was fascinated by fishing and bullfighting, subjects he explored many times in his writing. Photographers have similar obsessions, subjects that draw them back again and again: dogs, toddlers, drag queens, spiderwebs, lighthouses, dilapidated barns . . .

I've always felt a powerful attraction to water. Waterless parts of the world make me feel claustrophobic. I can never breathe easy in landlocked places. To feel truly at ease, I need proximity to ponds, marshes, lakes, rivers, and especially the ocean.

I love to photograph water. That's where I find my magic, especially in the interplay between water and light. I'm a sucker for a lovely reflection. Sure, other subjects catch my eye from time to time, but reflections have been my long-term fixation. I'm mesmerized by reflections of boats, birds, people,

Blue Jay

buildings, dock pilings, and clouds. I love the restless dance between object and its reflected doppelgänger. At times it's the reflection's mirrorlike accuracy that enthralls me, like the uncanny resemblance you see between identical twins, as with this photograph of a blue jay.

Other times it's the way a reflection will playfully distort the original image, often to the point where it is no longer recognizable though still striking in its own way.

Reflection feels like a metaphor. It reminds me of the duality of the world (if that doesn't sound too pretentious): up and down, dark and light, life and death. If you take a yoga class you may hear the instructor talk about *pose* and *counterpose*—for instance, arching forward, then arching back. In the yoga world, pose and counterpose balance each other and put you in harmony.

**Fishing Dock,
Key West**

Taking pictures feels like a refreshing counterpose to all the word work I've done for the past umpteen years. For most of my career I've been "all in" for words. Photography represents a seismic shift. My head isn't crammed with words when I sit by a tidal river, scouring the surface for wildlife. Instead it's awash with light, color, shape, and shadow. It feels like another portion of my brain switches on and starts humming. The part of my brain involved with language goes off-line for a little while.

Don Murray once remarked that a memoir represents a kind of reflection. It allows the writer to experience an event for a second time, by thinking and then writing about it. In his book *My Twice-Lived Life,* Murray (2001) says: "As life raced forward I would have to live backwards, the good and the bad, to remember what I had to forget and to celebrate so much that was good but had been passed by in the rush of life or passed over as ordinary when it was not."

Photographic reflections do something similar. You see the object once and then, a split second later, you see the reflection, tethered to the original image.

Often distortions in the reflection reveal something about the original you might not have noticed, exaggerating it in a way that makes you understand it for the first time.

The central metaphor of this book involves ways in which the craft of photography mirrors the craft of writing. Both activities involve the creative process. Both involve self-expression. Both allow an individual to represent a slice of the world and comment upon it. Both require craft/technique to be successful. As we will see, the language of photography—a language that is modern and tangible—has a great deal in common with the language of writing.

A series of savvy decisions are required to produce a memorable photograph. That's true with writing, as well. Understanding these decisions, and the options available to you, will help you take better pictures. And in our parallel universe (the world of writing), smart decisions about focus, detail, point of view, and so on create more effective writing.

Reflection is not an exact science; there's always an element of surprise. That's what makes it so fascinating. I was lucky enough to go to Abisko, Sweden, to photograph the northern lights. Before the trip I happened to run into Frank Serafini—friend, educator, and skilled photographer—and mentioned this upcoming trip.

"Try to find a place where you can get a reflection of the northern lights," Frank suggested.

"Are you serious?" I laughed out loud. "I'm going to a place above the Arctic Circle. It's going to be thirty degrees below zero! Where will I possibly find a reflection?"

"Just keep a lookout," he replied.

The weather predictions turned out to be accurate; temps hovered around −35° Fahrenheit. Sarah Skinner, a British photographer, led our trip. We photographed for three hours each night, from 8:30 to 11:30 P.M. Fortunately there was a "warming tent" where we could duck out of the cold. The first two nights yielded only teasing glimpses of the northern lights, but on the third night the heavens blossomed. An aurora curtain appeared, streaked with fantastic greens and pinks, arcing from one side of the sky to the other. I was speechless. Nothing in my life had prepared me for that moment.

As for trying to photograph this phenomenon, well, I was far out of my comfort zone. The sky turned so bright so quickly I couldn't figure out the right exposure. The shots I saw in the viewfinder of my camera were badly overexposed. Other photographers in our group had the same problem. We all started simultaneously peppering Sarah Skinner, our trip leader, with questions:

Northern Lights,
Abisko, Sweden

"What settings should I use?"

"Stop photographing!" she finally ordered. "Everybody, put down your camera for a few minutes. Just watch!"

Wise words. Too often an obsession with getting the shot interferes with the actual real-time experience. For the next twenty minutes we followed her suggestion. We gazed up at the sky, trying to absorb the spectacle we were witnessing.

Thirty minutes later the skies finally calmed down, still brilliant but no longer changing so rapidly. Sarah led us through a field of crunchy snow to a frozen pond a short distance away. I followed her with my camera and tripod and . . . there it was! There green aurora was reflected on the smooth ice—the very *last* thing I expected to see. Surprise, surprise, Frank Serafini, your advice turned out to helpful after all.

PART TWO

The Classroom

Craft Lessons

HOW TO USE THESE LESSONS

JoAnn Portalupi is my wife and coauthor; the craft lesson is our brainchild (Fletcher and Portalupi 2007). We wanted to create pithy, streamlined, high-quality lessons with practical ideas that would stretch young writers. The craft lessons in this section have been created with the same spirit. These lessons draw on the photographic world and build on links between photography (images) and writing (text). They apply to photography and writing and, hopefully, illuminate them both.

Each craft lesson has a section about photography followed by the Writing Connection (a discussion of the craft element in writing). These lessons have been designed to fit into the minilesson portion of your writer's workshop. Here are a few suggestions about how to use them:

1. Take a few minutes and read the lesson ahead of time. It will work best if you've got a clear grasp of the lesson's arc and flow.

2. First talk to students about what the craft element looks like in photography. <u>The actual text is intended as a guideline for the lesson—not a script to be read out loud</u>. Use language that feels comfortable to you.

3. Show students the photograph(s) in the lesson. After they have looked at it, give them a few minutes to turn and talk about what they see.

4. Segue from the craft element in photography to what this element looks like in writing. This transition may feel bumpy at first, but after the first few lessons you and your students will get used to it.

5. Read aloud the writing sample found in the Writing Connection part of the lesson.

6. Invite students to experiment with the craft element in their writing.

It's important that we, as writing teachers, supply rich ideas (strategies, techniques, craft moves) to stretch our students as writers. I would not expect every kid to use the craft element I teach. However, I usually highlight at least one student who tried the new craft lesson. If you have a share session at the end of the writing time, I suggest you select one student who tried the strategy of the day. You have a better chance of bringing these strategies to all your students if they can see their peers using them.

The best teaching often comes at the point of our own learning. I hope you'll bring these lessons into your classroom with a sense of adventure and a generous spirit. Expect the unexpected, as Don Murray would say (Murray 1989). Be alive to the little surprises you'll encounter along the way.

How to Access Online Resources

All of the photos in this book are available online. To access them go to:

http://hein.pub/focuslessons-login

Log in with your username and password. If you do not already have an account with Heinemann, you will need to create an account.

On the Welcome page, choose "Click here to register an Online Resource."

Register your product by entering the code: RFPHOTO (be sure to read and check the acknowledgment box under the keycode).

Once you have registered your product, it will appear alphabetically in your account list of My Online Resources.

Note: When returning to Heinemann.com to access your previously registered products, simply log into your Heinemann account and click on "View my registered Online Resources."

1 BEWARE THE *SO WHAT?* PRETTY PICTURE

People like to photograph pretty things: puppies, mountain vistas, a field of flowers. Those are the photos that grab our attention. Those are the pictures that get bought, framed, and hung on the wall. A photo of a tarantula gorging on a fly or an eviscerated dead seal washed up on a beach? Not so much.

Sunset photos fit this bill. You can find sunset photos in magazines, print ads, newspapers, screensavers, doctor's offices . . . Here's a sunset photo I took when visiting southeast Asia.

Sunset in Kolanta

There's nothing wrong with this picture. I do love that glowing pink light and the way the clouds are reflected in the wet sand. The line of boats marks the transition between sea and sky and enhances the tranquil mood. I'd love to take a stroll on that beach right now. And yet . . . haven't we seen this before?

Photographs like this are pretty but predictable; they run the risk of being little more than visual clichés. I don't mean to come off as a photo snob. Sure, there will always be a place for pretty pictures, but don't we hope to create images that do more than that? In Lesson 10 we'll see how incorporating one more element—a surprise splash in the water, the silhouette of an old man walking with a cane—can lift a photo like this into something truly memorable.

PHOTO TIP Be ruthless when you review your images. You do not need twenty identical images of the same pleasant picture. Take the one or two best ones, and delete the rest. You'll thank yourself later when you don't have to slog through umpteen images that are exactly alike.

Many writers create "pretty-picture" stories. They contain a happy beginning, happy middle, and a happy ending. The overall tone is resolutely upbeat:

> My Dad took me and my brother to Look Park. We had lots of fun. At first there weren't any kids there so we had the whole place to ourselves. We played Star Wars on the climbing structure. I was Han Solo. My brother was Chewbacca. Then we played hide and seek. Then two other kids came, a brother and sister. They wanted to play hide and seek with us, so we let them play. We had fun. The girl was good at hiding. When Dad said it was time to go home, none of us wanted to leave.

You can find stories like this every day in writing classrooms everywhere. When I read a piece like this I always have the same reaction: *So what?* I would probably not say this out loud (such a comment might come across as unfriendly or even hostile), but it's exactly what goes through my mind. I'm wondering: *Why does this experience matter to you? Or does it? Was this event important? Why should I care about this?*

In a stronger piece of writing the significance reveals itself; we find out why the writer chose to write about this. Maybe it's the first time Dad ever brought them to the park. Perhaps his brother has been sick, and it's the first outing since he came out of the hospital. Or maybe while playing with his brother he suddenly realized that . . .

This lesson is a cautionary tale for writers about what *not* to do. Beware the pretty-picture story because readers have little patience for them. Stories involve trouble. Something happens. Something goes wrong. Chaos crashes the party. A secret is uncovered. Dad, who has been super-stressed out at work, takes the family to a restaurant where he finds a dead fly in his vanilla pudding. Abruptly he stands up, spilling glasses at the table, blind with rage. Now the story gets interesting.

2 CONSIDER THE POINT OF VIEW

In Key West, Florida I took a class in travel photography led by David H. Wells. The course lasted only two and a half days, but our instructor packed a lot into it.

"Try changing your angle, or point of view, when you take photos," David advised on the first day. "Experiment by getting high like a giraffe, or low like a dog."

This advice may seem obvious, but I'd never thought much about what camera angle to use when taking pictures. Over the next few days I experimented with this technique. Later, when I was back in New Hampshire, I was standing on the back porch when I spotted my daughter-in-law and her youngest son directly below me. It was an unusual perspective, something you don't see every day. I grabbed my camera and snapped a few images.

Mother and Son

Many wildlife photographers teach the virtues of getting low (i.e., shooting a picture at the same level of your subject). This advice is harder than it sounds. It can be a challenge to crouch down low when you have creaky knees. Taking pictures from a prone position, when you're flat on the ground, often results in muddy clothes. Is it really worth it?

Well, yes. I've taken two photo trips with Glenn Bartley, a renowned bird photographer. On both trips Glenn emphasized the advantages of staying low when photographing birds:

- a better, cleaner background
- a sense that you're "in their world"
- dreamy foreground.

"When you get low, you make yourself small," Glenn added. "After a while the birds stop noticing you. When they become less afraid they often swim closer. That's a huge benefit to any photographer."

Mallard Duck

If your subject is on the ground or floating in the water, try not to shoot down. Instead, sit or lie down. In the duck photo, the bird's eye is level with the eye of the camera. That's something I try to do whenever photographing wildlife—I want my camera at eye level with the subject. This can make the photo feel more intimate. (Getting eye level with your subject isn't always possible, for instance, if you're photographing an owl perched on a branch twenty feet in the air.)

PHOTO TIP This advice applies not only to photographing wildlife but anything close to the ground: flowers, pets, small children. Don't shoot down on a toddler who is crawling or walking around you. Instead, sit down nearby. Lie down, if you can manage it. Now you are seeing things from her eye level, as she sees them. Sit quietly. After a while she'll forget you are there. Get your camera ready.

Solomon at the Playground

Writing Connection

Consider the words *point of view*. That familiar phrase reminds us that writers, like photographers, are image makers. Writers create mind pictures that allow the reader to see what's going on. A writer must decide: Whom do I want readers to focus on? What do I want them to see? And who is doing the seeing? Take this story:

> When I came into the living room the two little rug rats were lying on the rug, side by side, like two little slugs. One was trying to mash

two trucks together. The other one was laughing at who knows what. His belly jiggled when he giggled. I took a moment to survey wreckage. Seriously, it looked like someone had broken in and trashed the house. Blocks, Legos, trucks, wooden train track pieces were scattered everywhere. There was a pile of raisins next to them. Who was going to clean up this mess? I knew only too well the answer to that question.

In this snippet the author is "writing down" on the twins. I don't mean to suggest that the tone is condescending (it's not). The point of view is from an older person, perhaps a teenage babysitter, looking the children and the room around them. The same scene could have been written from a different point of view:

Rug is nice. It's soft like Mommy. Mommy's not here but I can stay on this nice Rug with Brother. Brother is nice. Brother makes funny faces. He makes me laugh. But sometimes Brother takes my Food and that's not nice. I have Rug and Toys and Brother and Little Black Things. I put a Little Black Thing in my mouth and it tastes so so good. Soft and squishy and Sweet Sweet Sweet. Brother will take the Little Black Things if he sees them but I don't want him to take them. Because they are Sweet. I will put all the Little Black Things in my mouth at the same time so Brother can't eat them.

Same scene, but a completely different point of view. Here I'm not writing down at the toddler; rather, I'm writing low, writing at his level, trying to enter his world as he might see it and bring it alive. One point of view is not better than the other—it depends on where you want readers to focus their attention.

Think about what point of view you want to take today when you write. The decision about point of view hinges on a fundamental question: Whose story is it? Whose fate is at stake? The toddler's? The babysitter's? The mother's? The answer to this question will determine the point of view you decide to take.

Violet Sabrewing

Photographs allow us to drink in the world. Most people don't want to sit in the nosebleed section. Give us seats in the front row. We want to lean in so we can see the sweat on LeBron James' brow.

Want to take better pictures? Don't hang back. Get closer. OK, so maybe right now you can't afford that expensive telephoto lens you've been coveting. That's no excuse. Get up and move closer.

"Your feet are your best zoom lens," photographer David Wells says. "I rarely crop my photos. I always try to move as close as possible."

Getting close to your subject gives you a fighting chance to capture the details viewers hunger for. I've long been fascinated by the hawk moth. This strange creature appears to be half insect and half hummingbird and shows up in our garden every summer. I took some photos and, later, shared them with my son Adam.

"A shot like this really changes the way you see," he said. "Look at that curly thing in front. It's covered in pollen."

Hawk Moth

PHOTO TIPS

- Plan ahead of time. Let's say you hope to photograph a whale—or a bride. Think carefully about what details you hope to capture. Eyes? Dress? Bridal veil? Baleen?

- Make sure you understand how to use the automatic focus (and other settings) on your camera. You don't want to be fiddling with your camera in the heat of the moment.

- Make sure your shutter speed is fast enough. Your photos will be blurred if your shutter speed is too slow.

Adam's right: photographs permanently alter the way we see and comprehend the world (see Chapter 6). A photo of the hawk moth reveals the fact that its body is surprisingly thick, shaped like a lobster, something I'd never noticed with my naked eye. Looking at photos often leads to these minidiscoveries. Perhaps you've watched hummingbirds flit through in your garden. If you study the close-up photo on page 41, you might notice that the feather pattern very much resembles the scales of a fish.

Writing Connection

Young writers often take a "soft focus." They write in generalities and don't pull in close. In fact, a story about an everyday event—eating lobster, putting a worm on a hook, wiping the face of your baby brother—can come alive if the writer pulls in close and uses precise description.

In my young adult novel, *The One O'Clock Chop* (2007), the main character is digging clams when he pulls something heavy from the bottom. It turns out to be a (gulp) dead body. I decided to pull in close to describe it:

I'd never seen a dead body before, and the drowned corpse looked pretty gruesome—the too-white skin, the man's tongue hanging out like a strip of wide, soggy ribbon. There was a strand of seaweed on the chin. I stared at the mouth. (7)

The first seven words are literally true. I wanted to "write small," but I had never seen the corpse of a drowned person, so I had to use my imagination. What would the skin look like? The tongue?

Elizabeth, a fifth grader, went on a trip to visit her great-grandmother in Guatemala. Notice the vivid detail she uses to make the story come alive.

I woke to the smell of tortillas being made. I slowly stepped onto the cool tile floor as I crept around the wooden dresser and out the door. I went into the kitchen to find Mama Lita, my great-grandma, making tortillas with my mom. Mama Lita saw me in the corner and asked (in Spanish): "Do you want to help me make tortillas?" I nodded and hurried into the kitchen. She explained the process. I tried to keep up with her but couldn't since I didn't understand Spanish that well. Instead, I watched her carefully and put together bits and pieces . . . I helped her make them, slowly putting one ingredient in after the other, and laughing with her as she told jokes.

Here are a few tips to share with young writers.

- Reread your writing and look for one or two places where the writing needs details to help the reader can picture what's going on. What details could you add that would strengthen it?

- Crack open general words like *fun*, *stuff*, *presents*. Use specific words instead: *arm wrestling, a brand-new baseball glove, the lingering smell of fried onions in the kitchen*. **The writing becomes beautiful when it becomes specific.**

- If you can't remember specific details about an event, give yourself permission to invent them. I did that many times when I wrote *Marshfield Dreams: When I Was a Kid* (2015) and *Marshfield Memories: More Stories About Growing Up* (2018).

- Use tiny details to reveal larger truths. "The bigger the issue, the smaller you write." Richard Price, novelist and screenwriter, shared this advice during a graduate writing class I took with him many years ago. These wise words inspire me even today.

PHOTO TIP Think small. Lesson 8 has more ideas about zooming in.

CAUTION: Move nearer to your subject, but not so close that you freak out wild animals. Great blue herons have been known to completely abandon a rookery due to human disturbance. I've heard many stories about over-zealous individuals trying to take a selfie with a buffalo or black bear. Bad idea. Be respectful. Use common sense.

PHOTO TIP It's helpful to show your pictures to a sympathetic friend. Ideally you want someone who can be supportive but can also offer a friendly critique (not someone who adores every single picture you take). My wife, JoAnn, has played that role for me. Often she sees something in a picture that totally escapes me. I don't always agree with her, but her response has helped me develop my own aesthetic and deepen my sense of what makes a strong image.

4 BRING SOMETHING STRONG

While visiting Port Townsend, Washington, I got up early and walked down to the dock with my camera. I spent forty-five minutes taking pictures of pigeon guillemots. They flew at rapid speed, zooming in for awkward landings. I swiveled my camera this way and that, but the light was murky, and it was next to impossible to get the birds in focus. The resulting pictures didn't thrill me. I deleted most of them, though I kept a few marginal images, including this one:

Pigeon Guillemot

I certainly wasn't wowed by this picture. The bird's body is not in sharp focus. You can't see much detail on the feathers. But when I showed it to a friend he laughed in delight: "Ha! Look at those feet! You even caught the reflection!"

This surprised me. Other people had a similar reaction, so I finally decided to stop hating on this photo. No, the picture is not perfect, but it works in its own way. I learned something that day: one striking detail or strong element can redeem an otherwise ordinary picture.

Amanda's third-grade teacher invited her students to write poems. It was hard for Amanda at first, but eventually she came up with this:

Baking Day

When Daddy says we're baking blueberry muffins

I know I'm in for a treat.

He piles the ingredients on the counter:

flour, brown sugar, vanilla, baking soda, blueberries.

I sneak some berries into my mouth

while I mix the batter.

Daddy pours out just enough

for each baking cup.

After we slide the pans in the oven

I wipe down the counter.

Then it's time to wait.

Before too long the

sweet muffiny smell

fills the whole house with joy.

Amanda's writing is typical of what you might see from students in third grade. It certainly has some strengths, including details and focus. She creates a sense of anticipation. But in most ways it's rather ordinary . . . until: "Before too long the sweet muffiny smell fills the whole house with joy." I love how she situates this wonderful line at the very end where it can echo in the reader's mind. The lesson here is that one memorable line can redeem an otherwise ordinary piece of writing. It doesn't have to be exceptional from beginning to end, but there needs to be something strong for the reader to grab onto.

"In our images we're competing for the scarce and precious attention of viewers," photographer Guy Tal says. "If an image doesn't engage their minds in a meaningful way, they will divert their attention to things they deem more worthy. This is where visual tension comes in. Tension is what prompts the viewer's brain to spend a little extra attention trying to understand an image" (Tal 2018).

Guy Tal reminds us that we can never take the attention of the viewer (or the reader) for granted. Incorporating tension in your photographs might seem like a daunting task, but it's not as hard as it might first seem.

Artists talk about dynamic tension, including elements that clash or pull the viewer in two different directions. This photograph of the Flume Gorge in New Hampshire shows huge slabs of ancient granite juxtaposed with flowing water. The contrast between the rock and the water creates drama. By using a slow shutter speed, I was able to give the water a feathery quality, which sharpens the contrast.

The Flume Gorge, New Hampshire

You can also feel tension in the street scene (below), a photo I took in Hội An, Vietnam. Here we see a man sitting on the ground while repairing a bicycle. The woman sitting nearby doesn't look someone who does manual labor. She crouches a few inches from the ground, wearing makeup, lipstick, and high heels. The two struck me as an incongruous couple, something you wouldn't likely see in our country.

■ Beware placing your subject in the exact center of the picture. This creates a static image. Experiment with situating your subject to one side of the picture or another.

■ Be on the lookout for visual contrast—a tall father dancing with his little daughter at the wedding.

■ Incorporate something surprising or incongruous that might make viewers do a double take and spend more time looking at your photo.

Street Scene in Hội An, Vietnam

Another way of creating tension is to freeze the action not at the climactic moment but immediately *before* something important occurs—right before bride and groom kiss, for example. This makes a space for the viewer to take part in the unfolding drama. The photo on the next page shows a great blue

Great Blue Heron on the Prowl

heron hunting for food. The carefully raised foot reveals his purpose and intense concentration. The sharp beak is like a bow drawn back. We anticipate the action about to occur—the foot will come down, the beak will dart forward, the fish will be snared—even though we never actually see the resolution.

Writing Connection

Tension matters in writing, as well. It's not simply a nice idea to incorporate tension—it's essential. Something must make the reader want to keep reading: a mystery must be solved, a question must be answered, the end of the story must be revealed. (Will the father of the injured son forgive the policeman who shot him . . . or not?)

> Finally, the happy day arrived—my big sister's wedding—though the mood at our house didn't feel happy. The weather broke bright and sunny. All morning Mom and Dad stayed busy with preparations for the reception, though I never saw them talking with each other. My cousins helped Mom set up the chairs. My uncles helped Dad stack booze and ice at the bar. In the early afternoon they brought in the flower arrangements.
>
> "How beautiful!!" Mom exclaimed. But her eyes lacked their usual sparkle. I noticed tight little frown marks at the corner of her mouth.

In this snippet you sense something wrong—bad blood between the parents. We note the contrast between a joyful event (receiving fresh flowers) and the frown lines on Mom's face. The tension makes the reader push ahead to find answers to the following questions:

- What is the source of the tension?

- Will it get better or worse?

- Will it impact the nuptials?

Make sure you incorporate tension in your writing. And don't wait too long to do it—we should feel that tension early on. The reader should hear the roar of the waterfall from the very first paragraph. Remember:

- Stories are about trouble. Usually the trouble gets worse before it gets better.

- In grappling with the difficult situation, the main character often learns something about him- or herself.

- Characters should do more than reflect—we want to see them *react*. That reaction creates conflict, which in turn ratchets up the tension and the drama. That's what readers hunger for.

6   PLAY WITH FOREGROUND AND BACKGROUND

Most people who take pictures focus on the subject to the exclusion of everything else. But it's important to consider all the elements that go into creating an image:

- ◆ foreground—anything that lies between you and your subject
- ◆ midground—typically (though not always) where you place your subject
- ◆ background—everything behind the subject.

A photograph might be compared to a stage. The "upstage" holds the background and provides a setting for the story. Center stage is where most of the action takes place. Downstage—foreground—is closest to the audience. It's helpful to be aware of those three elements when you're taking pictures.

I took this photo in Lubec, Maine. I have taken umpteen photos at this spot, but this one stands out. In this picture the foreground, midground, and background create three distinct layers. There's a pleasing tension (as discussed in the previous lesson) between the colors. The presence of blue and white clouds in the background make the gold seaweed pop. The seaweed wouldn't be as striking if photographed all by itself. Also, the presence of the midground (water) and background (sky) gives the photo depth. When looking at this photograph you feel as though you're looking across a distance.

Tidal River, Downeast Maine

Aaron and JoAnn

It's important to consider background and foreground when photographing people, too. My grandson Aaron was my subject in this photo, but including JoAnn in the background adds another dimension. It's more than a portait of a beaming boy—her presence deepens the image by reminding us of the connections between family generations.

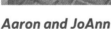

Writing Connection

Foreground and background can open up dramatic new possibilities for any piece of writing:

> Today the legal drinking age in New York State is twenty-one. Before 1985 you could legally drink at nineteen. In the years prior to 1982 you could drink at eighteen. No wonder alcohol-related traffic deaths remained sky-high in the mid-1970s. In 1974 the

number of New Yorkers who died in car crashes totaled 6,831. That sounds like just one more boring number, but one of them was my brother.

October 18, 1974. Friday night. My parents were home watching TV. Bobby was out with his friends Scott Montgomery and Johnny Jones. They started the evening drinking beer at the Copper Kettle, a popular bar. Bobby was only seventeen, but he had a fake ID card. The other guys did too. Back then fake IDs were easy to get; the bouncers didn't look too hard. At the bar somebody mentioned a party on Sequams Lane, so the boys quickly finished their beers and climbed back into the car. Johnny was driving; Bobby was sitting next to him. "Smoke on the Water" by Deep Purple blasted from the radio. Nobody wore seatbelts.

In this piece the first paragraph provides a background or backdrop. Impersonal facts set up the personal tragedy that follows. The statistics give the reader a wider context and deepen our understanding of what happened next. The background, or introduction, is often found at the beginning of a piece of writing, but it can also appear at the end of a piece, as in "On the Back of the Bus" (Fletcher 2018, 151).

Think about foreground and background as you work on your writing. Would including background information strengthen the story you want to tell or the argument you want to make? If so, consider adding this to your writing.

7 TAKE A WIDE PERSPECTIVE

Pulling in close is usually a smart idea when you're taking pictures, but not always. Sometimes a tight focus makes the viewer feel claustrophobic. The viewer may hunger for a wider view: a beach panorama, the mountains at twilight, an immense crowd at a college football game.

I took the following photo at a tidal river in Downeast Maine on a warm summer night. I was entranced by the sight of the stars reflected in the glassy water. Instead of zooming in on one celestial body or constellation, I wanted to try to capture the whole scene: river, dark islands, luminous stars. Luckily there was no wind, but even so it wasn't an easy picture to take. I had to adjust the settings on the back of my camera in near-darkness . . . all the while awkwardly perched on a craggy rock. And I had to keep the camera still for a twenty- or twenty-five-second exposure. But I was pleased with the result, especially the reflection of the Milky Way itself.

PHOTO TIP As its name implies, a wide-angle lens will allow you to capture a wider perspective. However, you don't necessarily have to buy a specialized lens for that purpose. Most smartphone cameras come already outfitted with a wide-angle lens.

A River of Stars

Whenever you're taking pictures, you need to ask yourself: should I pull back and give the viewer a wider sense of what's going on? Sometimes it makes sense to "go wide." A wide-angle view has several advantages:

- It is great for landscape photography.

- It shows the subject not in isolation but in the context of his or her world, in relation to others.

- It allows you to make a panorama by stitching photos together later.

Writing Connection

Writing teachers often encourage students to "write small," to select a "slice of the pizza." But a wide-angle focus can be just as useful in writing as it is in photography. Sometimes we want to take a broader focus. In the following poem, I decided not to zero in on any one person. The subject is the sprawling family and the narrator's dawning awareness about his connection to a larger clan.

Family Photo

One last picture
before we head off
in different directions.

One last group of
all of us, smirking,
with rabbit ears.

Three generations,
kids on shoulders,
a baby cousin on my lap.

And in the middle
Grandma and Grandpa
who started all this.

We're all ripples in a pond
spreading out
from a stone they threw.

Today when you write, ask yourself: do I want to zoom in or take a wide-angle focus? Caution: when you "go wide" in writing there's a tendency to create a list. Lists tend to be tedious; they suck the drama out of the writing. Notice how the last stanza in "Family Photo" breaks the list pattern and pulls the poem together with a metaphor (ripples in a pond).

Red-Legged Tree Frog

PHOTO TIP When you pull in close, it can be hard to get the whole subject in perfect focus. Never forget the most important part: the eyes. Viewers can live with a slightly out of focus wing or bridal veil, but not the eyes. Work hard to get a sharp focus on the eyes.

By zooming in, you invite viewers to move from the middle of the theater and sit in the front row. Now they can drink up all those tantalizing details: the elaborate braid pattern on the snake, or the bright bulbous eye in this tree frog (above).

It's true that a close focus may come at a cost. Zoom in too close and you pull the subject out of its natural habitat. Stripped of all reference points, the subject can seem isolated. I was glad to be able to show this tree frog in a tropical elephant leaf. Even so we have no other visuals to compare it to, and we don't know how big this leaf is, so there's no way to tell the size of this frog.

Remember: Be respectful of your subject, especially when using flash. Give animals and people as much space as possible. Be on the lookout for signs you are stressing them out—if you notice that happening, back off.

Shrewd writers know that less is often better when you are describing people and places. You don't need to describe everything about your subject. You can bring alive a character by zooming in and focusing on one aspect, gesture, or feature.

> Uncle Jack has squinty blue eyes, fat cheeks, and silver hair cut short, military-style. But it's his nose that he's famous for. He's got a big beak, a true schnozz, an old-fashioned honker that jumps out and practically mugs you when he looks in your direction. You can't help staring at that big slab of meat. His nose is crooked; the story goes that he broke it in a bar fight back in the day, and the doctor didn't set it properly. But Uncle Jack doesn't mind if people stare. "My mother gave me this can-opener when I was born," he says with a twisted grin, "so I guess I'm stuck with it."

In this portrait I could have talked about Uncle Jack's military career. I could have described his bulk, beer belly, or bull neck. Instead I decided to emphasize one facial feature: his nose. I am trusting my readers. I know if I do a good enough job describing one aspect of this man, readers will be able to fill in the rest.

Be strategic when you zoom in. Don't waste your time describing a trivial aspect of your subject. Pick something that's representative or emblematic of the larger whole. And try to find some unusual or surprising detail (that nose set at a crooked angle) that will stick in the reader's mind.

Mood is rooted in emotion. Mood makes us feel nostalgic, angry, celebratory, etc. If you hope to convey a specific mood in a photograph, you have to feel it yourself first.

In late October I got up early to photograph at Adam's Point, a coastal area in Durham, New Hampshire. I drove to one spot that has ocean on one side and a marsh on the other. Those are usually promising conditions for spotting birds, but today when I climbed out of my car nothing seemed to be moving. I connected the camera to my tripod and waited. Still nothing. I let my eyes wander, roaming near and far over ocean and marsh. A few hundred yards offshore I noticed a blanket of mist rising off the ocean. Just then the sun came out, illuminating the mist directly behind the boat. The sight of that boat, still bathed in shadow, with the bright mist behind it gave me a thoughtful, peaceful feeling. The photo below captures that mood. I like the way the boat engine on the right is counterbalanced by the cormorant on the left.

Early Morning at Adam's Point

PHOTO TIPS

■ Think about color. Color is important for establishing mood of an image. Dark, muted colors give a feeling of reflection, sadness, or calm. Bright vibrant colors suggest excitement/ happiness.

■ Keep an eye on the weather. Photographer David Pritchett has this advice: "To get the best shots, you need to wait until there is a break in the weather to get some really interesting lighting effects from the turbulent sky. It's more of a challenge to portray mood on bright, sunny, cloudless days" (2019).

In the next photo, the two tree limbs frame the egret's head. Notice that the egret's head is in focus; everything else is blurred. This creates a mood of heightened drama and anticipation.

Egret in the Everglades

Writing Connection

Mood is not just a consideration for photos—it's equally important when you're writing.

"Mood is the glue that holds all the arts together," says Trevor Bryan, author of *The Art of Comprehension* (2019). "It's how we connect to stories and poems."

I'm acutely conscious of mood in my writing. At the beginning of my novel *Spider Boy* (1997), the main character has moved from Illinois to New York and isn't happy about it. Bobby has left his good friends behind—he feels dislocated. I wanted to convey the sense of a boy who is not "at home" in his world.

> After Bobby hung up he went to his bedroom. He looked around at all the boxes containing his stuff, the posters still rolled up. It looked like he just arrived yesterday. The only thing he had unpacked were his clothes and a few books. The room was long and narrow. With the walls bare, you could see that they needed a

paint job. There were four windows, each shaped like a quarter of a circle. Those windows, Mom said, gave the room character: Four quarters equals a whole. But it didn't add up.

He lay back on his bed. The house was perfectly quiet, as if all human sound had been sucked forever from those four walls. (20)

I deliberately chose details (bare walls, rolled-up posters, eerie silence) to show that Bobby has not settled in to his new house.

Mood should be more than a relish or condiment—it's fundamental to the work and should be a basic consideration for any piece of writing. If you're going to write a scene about getting ready for a backyard wedding reception you need to imagine the prevailing mood around the house. Happy? Tense? Chaotic? How might you describe the characters or setting to best convey that mood to your readers?

10 INCLUDE AN EXTRA ELEMENT

Colorful bird photos? I've only got a few thousand. But the ones that stand out are often the pictures that include something extra—a bird not in isolation but *nestled with one of its chicks*. The extra element gives the viewer a wider sense of the bird's life, its daily routine, the challenges it faces. Very often this "plus one" feature makes a photograph come alive.

Gulls are common as pine cones in coastal Maine, so much so they're practically invisible to me. ("That's not a bird," I mutter when I see one, "it's just a gull.") I took the following photograph in Maine. This picture reveals one of the many ways gulls feed themselves, working the muddy flats at low tide, pulling up sea worms, and gulping them down like fresh pasta. The herring gull has turned to us, showing its prize. The worm is quite prominent . . . you could almost say it's a photograph of a worm that has been caught by a gull. Notice that the gull's grip on the worm doesn't seem very firm. He holds it casually, making us wonder: will he drop it?

Herring Gull with Seaworm

I've taken many photos of my grandson Solomon, but this one is one of my favorites. His head is tilted, eyes dreamy, expression relaxed, a playful half smile on his face. You can see Solomon's tongue through the bubble, so you know he's tasting it. There's an undercurrent of tension: surely the fragile bubble will burst at any moment.

PHOTO TIP Don't be too aggressive when you crop your photos. Often the original image includes an interesting "plus one" element (for instance, the bicycle helmet in the photo at left) that gets eliminated if we crop the image too tightly. Doing so may actually weaken the image.

"I wonder what bubbles taste like . . ."

Writing Connection

It's helpful to incorporate another element or dimension when you have your characters interacting with each other. JoAnn and Martha are talking *while baking cookies*. I talk to my father *while bandaging his foot where he's just had a toe amputation . . . a wound that refuses to heal*. This allows us to see them in the larger world, interacting with their environment.

In my *The One O'Clock Chop* (2007), Matt (fifteen) gets his first job working with a clam digger named Dan. Each morning they climb onto Dan's boat to spend the day harvesting clams. Matt's father is absent, so Dan becomes a kind of father figure. They eventually have some meaningful conversations, but most of their early interactions involving hard, tedious work on the boat.

> At three forty-five I sat down on the deck, exhausted. I could barely lift my arms, let alone the tongs. My bushel basket was full, though.
> "How'd you do?" Dan asked.
> "A bushel," I said proudly.
> "Let's take a look." He took out a shallow box that had four metal bars on the bottom, evenly spaced. "First we gotta run 'em through the cull rack. Dump some in here."
> I hoisted the bushel basket and spilled about two dozen clams into the cull rack. It made a loud noise when Dan shook it, and five clams fell through the iron bars onto the deck.
> "Those are seed, baby clams," Dan explained, kicking them overboard. "They're tasty, melt in your mouth. But you gotta throw them back unless you're eager to pay a thousand-dollar fine to Conservation." (19)

Read over the places where you describe a character. Does your portrayal of that character feel accurate but lifeless? Try adding an extra element—a quirky detail, peculiar habit, routine or ritual—to make that character come alive.

11 EMBRACE SURPRISE

There's a small tidal creek in Machais, Maine, where I often stop to look for wildlife. One day I noticed a female merganser leading a string of chicks upstream. Seeing that ragged line of baby mergansers got me excited. I wanted to climb down and shoot the birds at eye level, but I didn't have time. The mother was swimming fast, and it was all I could do to grab a few shots. Later, when I looked at the images, I saw something I hadn't noticed before. Four of the chicks were swimming, but one chick had hopped onto its mother's back.

Merganser and Chicks

That one element—a lazy chick sitting contentedly on Mama's back—makes the photo, but I never anticipated it when I squeezed the shutter. Little surprises like that crop up frequently when you're taking pictures. Another time I had the opportunity to photograph the solar eclipse. I did a lot of research and planned it carefully. This photo (on page 64) succeeded in catching the "diamond ring" stage. Notice the fragment of a rainbow on the lower left, something I didn't see through the camera when I took this shot.

PHOTO TIP You can't guarantee that something surprising will happen, but you want to be ready in case it does. Keep your focus on your subject but, at the same time, try to be open to something unplanned and unexpected. A photograph has an uncanny ability to capture those spontaneous moments.

Solar Eclipse Diamond Ring Effect

Writing Connection

It seems to me the element of surprise in writing has largely been ignored, or even discouraged. Many schools promote a particular essay format: tell readers what you will tell them, then tell them, and finally tell them what you just told them. When students are directed to follow such a rigid sequence/formula, there's little opportunity for them to take advantage of the surprises that might arise.

The title of Don Murray's (1989) book—*Expecting the Unexpected*—reminds us that surprise is an integral part of the writing process. It's one of the ways we keep writing fresh. We write to find out what we don't know about what we know. Most writers report that the process they follow involves a great deal of discovery.

The poet X. J. Kennedy told a college class about the time he was writing a poem about food. When he looked up the word *strudel* in his rhyming dictionary he came across *poodle*. He ended up writing a poem about dogs—not at all what he'd intended.

"One of the things I like most about writing is finding a surprise in what I write," Paul Janeczko told me (email to author, May 27, 2018). "I often want my characters to zig but they want to zag. When I was writing my book, *Worlds Afire* [2007], I thought the characters would react one way to the fire, but they often wanted to go in another direction. In the final poem, I thought the speaker wouldn't want to watch the movie he had made of the fire. He insisted on watching it, but only once. And he really surprised me when, after he watched, he rewound it and saw that some of the victims were actually happy 'for the last time in their lives.'"

One implication is that we should be cautious about imposing a rigid prewriting form or making students rely too heavily on it. Writing involves an act of discovery, figuring out what you want to say. Flexibility is key. We want students to feel free to zag when they write, even if they had originally planned to zig.

Tell your students: today if you find yourself writing something unexpected or surprising, don't run away from it. Pause and consider. Experiment. You might decide to try a new draft, and see what happens if you allow your writing to go in a new direction.

PHOTO TIP You can reveal motion not only by what moves but also by the reaction caused by that motion. In the great egret photo, the exploding water shows us the speed and force of the strike.

12 SHOW MOTION

Video employs a rapid succession of images to show action or motion. A photo must somehow show motion using nothing but a single, fixed image. How?

The secret's in the shutter speed. You must use a shutter speed that's fast enough to capture the movement. Otherwise you end up with umpteen coulda-woulda-shoulda near-miss blurry images.

I spent a half hour watching this great egret wading in a pond. Conditions were promising: late afternoon, soft light, no wind to ruffle the surface of the pond. Although the egret looked quite regal and refined, I knew it was on a deadly mission. It struck with amazing speed, but I must have been using a slow shutter speed because the first dozen images I took all came out looking blurry. So, I jacked my shutter speed up to 1/1,250th of a second to get this picture. Now when the egret struck I was able to freeze its slender neck in sharp focus.

Great Egret Strikes

The egret photograph freezes one particular moment, but sometimes you want to show recurring or ongoing motion. I'm fascinated by hummingbirds' uncanny ability to hover in one place. It's a paradox of nature: it requires incredible motion (eighty wing flaps per second) for this bird to remain so still. Here the blurred wings convey the whirring motion while the upper part of the bird—particularly the eye—stays in focus.

Violet Sabrewing

Writing Connection

My Aunt Mary never married; to my knowledge she never even had a romantic friend. But she often related a story about one of the rare occasions when she went on a date. Her companion took her to a candlelit restaurant. He ordered a bottle of wine. But at one point in the evening he made an impudent remark.

"So, what did you do?" we asked eagerly, knowing what was coming next.

"I flung the wine in his face!" Mary said triumphantly.

I loved this story; my whole family did. We could clearly picture the sputtering man, his face drenched in wine. Was it true? Did she actually throw wine in his face? Well, possibly not, but that wasn't the point. It was a *story*. During her life my aunt did a great deal of tedious work for many unappreciative people. No doubt there were many occasions when she badly wanted to throw wine in someone's face. In this story she could finally do it.

Stories turn on a moment like that. Certainly, a story requires characters and setting, but the payoff is carried by action. In *Spider Boy*, Bobby gets tormented by another kid named Chick Hall. Eventually they get into a fistfight. I wanted to describe what it felt like when Bobby gets punched in the face. I forced myself to slow down and not rush the action.

> Bobby turned to Chick just in time to see a fist screaming toward his left eye. In that clear autumn light Bobby could see the punch arriving in perfect detail, the fist against Chick's white T-shirt, a line of white knuckles streaking toward his face—then BAM! Bobby went down, not with stars in his head the way it happened on cartoons but with bright streaks of dancing light. His head bounced heavily on the ground. The smell of grass filled nose. Dazed and nauseous, he got to his knees. Lunch rose in his belly. (1997, 137)

One of the best ways to bring your characters alive is to get them doing something, that is, catch them in motion. When describing action, keep a few things in mind:

- ◆ Show your character physically reacting, not reflecting.
- ◆ Use active verbs. Avoid passive verbs like *is*, *was*, *were*.
- ◆ You don't have to describe everything. Describe one or two details (the line of white knuckles) with enough detail so the reader can picture them.
- ◆ Don't speed through the action. Take your time. Think: slow motion.

In Dana's fifth-grade class, Drew wanted to write about how excited he felt when he got a new pet. Here's what he originally wrote: "I reached over and picked up the ball of fluff."

After Dana taught the "Show Motion" craft lesson, Drew decided to go back and revise that part of his writing. Note how he slows this moment and does a much better job of describing what happened: "I dropped my hands, tensing them, hoping he wouldn't be heavy. As my heart beat faster, I reached my hands under him and picked up the ball of fluff that started to squirm in my hands."

13 | DRAW IN THE VIEWER

Photographers strive to bring the viewer into the world captured by an image, but that's not as easy as it sounds. A photograph is a two-dimensional space usually bordered by four right angles. Given those constraints, how do you entice the viewer?

Try using a leading line. Photographer Joshua Cripps describes this compositional technique like this: "Leading lines draw the viewer into the photo, lead them on a journey through the image, and ultimately point them at some kind of visual payoff . . . Leading lines are generally most effective when they're diagonal or curving lines. These lines break up the square format of the photo, and help the viewer's eye traverse the entire frame" (Cripps 2016).

In the photograph of the northern lights (page 30), you'll notice two leading lines: the crack in the ice as well as the aurora's reflection. Both lines draw the viewer's eye to what's happening in the sky. In *Sunset on Cobscook Bay* (below) the shoreline creates a leading line that starts on the bottom left, and leads our eye to the sunset.

PHOTO TIP
Horizontal lines (lines that go left to right) do not work well to draw in a viewer and, in general, should be avoided. They can create a visual roadblock that prevents the viewer's eye from flowing into your image.

Sunset on Cobscook Bay

Next time you're taking pictures try experimenting with a leading line. Look through the viewer and break down what you see into abstract lines, not literal objects. This may sound complicated, but with practice you'll be able to do it. A road isn't a stretch of pavement, it's a series of parallel lines. A river isn't flowing water, it's a curving line snaking across the landscape. By moving your camera to the left or the right you can change where the leading line appears in your photo. (You can also do this by cropping it later.)

Writing Connection

Q: If the leading line is a useful compositional tool in photography, what's the corresponding move in writing?

A: The lead.

Skillful writers carefully craft a lead aimed at drawing readers into the piece. Lead-wise, writers have many options: the anecdote, tantalizing fact, sound effects, an allusion to mythology or pop culture. Here I'm going to model one strategy you might try.

> Did you ever experience crippling brain-freeze after eating too much ice cream too fast? Did you ever feel such intense head pain you had to crouch down so you wouldn't collapse on the sidewalk? You know this sensation will fade within twenty or thirty seconds. Just one of the annoyances of summer, right?
>
> Well, maybe not. Recent research suggests that the ice cream brain-freeze may not be as harmless as we assumed.

This lead uses a series of questions. I chose ones I figured readers would likely answer in the affirmative: *Oh yes, that has definitely happened to me. I know what it feels like.* Like the leading line in photography, these questions build a bridge between the reader's experience and the next point I want to make. They create common ground, a place where the reader and I can hopefully find agreement and stand together. They get the reader on board and in sync with me before I introduce my main point.

Think carefully about your lead when you write today. Consider using a series of questions to draw in the reader.

14 USE GESTURE TO REVEAL CHARACTER

Our gestures are as unique as our fingerprints or the sound of our voices. There are gestures we make only under certain circumstances—when we are stressed, happy, pensive, bored, or being mischievous.

"Often a gesture or an expression can be at the heart of a successful image," says William Allard, a *National Geographic* photographer.

Spaz Being Spaz

PHOTO TIP When sorting through photographs, there's a temptation to choose straight-forward portraits: facing the camera, smiling, in good light. Make sure to mark as "keepers" the ones that show your subject making a distinctive gesture—even ones the subject might consider awkward or unflattering. These are often the pictures we treasure the most.

How do we make sense of this photograph of Spaz? Our reaction will be partly based on the man's unusual look: dyed hair, collar, zany T-shirt. But Spaz's peculiar gesture also gives us important clues about what this man might be like. The same thing could be said of the following photo of JoAnn. The gesture suggests that she has a playful spirit.

Reaching the Summit

Writing Connection

Describing a gesture is an indispensable tool when it comes to creating character in writing. There's an old saying that *you can tell a more about a man by the way he butters his toast than by what he says.* But you don't just pick a random gesture to describe. Rather, you select one that reveals something important about the character.

> My big brother had long hair. He used to flick his head to get his hair out of his eyes. That was his signature move: flick, flick, flick. My parents figured he'd go to college, but he joined the Air Force instead. On the first day they shaved my brother's hair. When he came home with his buzz cut I burst out laughing. Mom said she liked it, and I guess it looked okay. But you know what? My brother still did that flick-flick-flicking thing with his head, even after his long hair was long gone.

Adam Myman, a fourth-grade teacher in California, tried this craft lesson with the young writers in his class. Here's what Simon came up with. His writing reminds us that the most effective gestures are often the ones that reflect what's going on (tension, exasperation, exultation) in the larger scene.

"Stop it!" Mom yelled at me and my brother to stop fighting. My brother started to solve his Rubik's cube very fast. He grinded his teeth. I looked at the ground and fiddled with my fingers.

My sister started cracking jokes and everyone except my brother laughed hysterically. My brother just started to solve it faster and faster. My sister kept on making jokes and there wasn't any more fighting. After a few minutes all we could hear was the music and the loud "Click-click-click" of the Rubik's cube. And that's all we heard until we got home.

PHOTO TIP Take an honest, unflinching look at the world around you, and if you see something that provokes a strong reaction in you—even if it's ugly—take out your camera and grab the shot. Resist the temptation to delete them when you review your images later. You'll be glad you preserved them.

15 | TELL THE TRUTH

In Kerala, India, I hired a local bird guide who promised to bring me to a place where I could photograph steppe eagles. I was excited; however, the setting turned out to be nothing like what I'd imagined. We arrived at a place full of reeking trash—a dump! Amid the rubbish, a half dozen bedraggled eagles were listlessly picking at scraps of food. I stared at the guide in disbelief.

"Is this the only place you've got where I can photograph steppe eagles?"

"It's not beautiful," he admitted, "but you said you wanted to see them. This is probably the place where you can be sure of finding them."

I didn't know what to say. Dazed, I pulled out my camera and took a few photos, but my heart wasn't in it. I couldn't get away from that place fast enough.

Steppe Eagle in Kerala, India

The bad taste in my mouth lingered all day. I felt angry that such a majestic creature had to spend its days in such a godawful place. I was sorely tempted to delete all the eagle photos I took that day, but I kept a few, including this one. And I'm glad I did because I think it's important. This image speaks to the destructive impact humans have had on this planet. I don't mean to single out India—the United States has been a major polluter, as well.

We love to photograph fresh flowers and fetching toddlers, but there's undeniable power in gritty photographs that reveal truths about our world:

- ◆ smoke pouring out of a smokestack
- ◆ angry faces at a demonstration
- ◆ an injured child being carried from earthquake rubble.

In the last 200 years photography has been a powerful and persuasive force to help people face hard truths: thalidomide babies, child labor, the meatpacking industry, the civil rights movement, just to name a few. It's not a matter of quantity, either. One or two disturbing photos played a pivotal role in turning the American public against the Vietnam War.

So be bold when you photograph. It sounds improbable but it's true: one photo can change the world.

Writing Connection

Tell your story.

You own everything that happened to you—the good, the bad, and everything in between. Write what really matters. What else is writing for? This craft lesson will serve as an antidote for superficial writing where you can tell students are not invested in what they're putting on paper.

The following piece was written by Eric, an eighth-grade student in Philadelphia. This young writer certainly doesn't pull any punches, and yet it's not shrill, either. He writes with honesty, but also uses a bit of humor. There's an underlying tone of wisdom and even tenderness.

Dedication

This is not the type of dedication you would expect to see. The person I dedicate this to never affected me like a normal person's father or mother. I dedicate this memoir to my father. My father in blood, not Sean my step-dad, who's been in my life as much if not more than my real dad. My dad left when I was six or seven, I can't really remember. He left his cats and told me he was going on a vacation. After a bit I realized he wasn't on vacation. Even though he is no longer family, he is at least my relative, and I want to say thank you to him. I know it's weird, but he showed me how to be independent. How to not be hurt when someone is not who I hope and want them to be. He gave me these three amazing cats but only one is left now. He gave me great hair and a great aunt who recently gave birth to my brand-new cousin. He gave me my skin color and my Asian descent, and gave me a great college essay topic. I recently saw him to renew my passport for a Costa Rica trip. And although there are all these thank yous . . . screw you for leaving and not saying goodbye, screw you for not texting or sending letters for six or seven years. Screw you for lying and not telling the truth. But especially, screw you for making my mom and my aunt's life harder and making her sad. Of course, I would never say any of this to anyone, I'm too nice. And he should be thankful, because I'm sure this would make him cry, it would put into the light what he's done, and what he hasn't done. Even though he's done these things, I'm still thankful for what he has given me and hope he can sort his life out and be a part of mine again.

What's Happening in This Photograph?

The fourth graders leaned in for a closer look.

"I can't see!" one kid objected. "Let me have a turn!"

The students were fixated on a photo that showed a young couple standing on top of a tall building with the Manhattan cityscape spread out behind them. The two people were smiling, oblivious to a commercial jet that was heading straight for the building where the couple was standing. The photo, titled *The Moment Before*, conjured up horrors of 9/11 and the destruction of the World Trade Center.

The picture hits you like a gut punch, but, of course, it was a hoax. The commercial jet had been Photoshopped into the image. It's a classic example of two legitimate images combined to create fake news. There's no shortage of counterfeit images like this one. But it should be noted that photos are often altered in smaller ways, with subtle changes barely detectable to the untrained eye. *Newsweek* ran a cover photo (May 18, 1970) of an anguished girl at Kent State University, her classmate sprawled on the ground. This image became iconic, an unforgettable reminder of the toll the war was taking on our country. In the original photo a fence post in the background protrudes from the girl's head.

Kent State Shooting, May 4, 1970

The photo editors probably thought it detracted from the power of the images, so they removed the fence post in the image that got published in the magazine (*Time* "Top 10 Doctored Photos").

You may counter: so what? The change was trivial. The essential truth of the photo—an unarmed college student killed by the U.S. National Guard—remains unchanged. To which I would reply: yes, that's true, but isn't this a slippery slope? If editors feel entitled to change one part of a photo for aesthetic reasons, what's to stop them from making more substantial changes? Indeed, this has happened many times in the last hundred years. And shouldn't this shake our belief in photographs as primary sources and unassailable purveyors of truth?

"We've come to expect that photographs reveal the truth of any historical moment," says Laura Smith, an archivist at the University of Connecticut. "We have to remember that photographs can be altered and obscured, which affects our knowledge of historical events" (Smith 2016).

You cannot take any photo at face value. Photographs can be misleading, and even accurate photos that have not been retouched convey meaning that isn't always self-evident. We need to help students become savvy consumers of the images that permeate our world. One problem is the human tendency to give photographs little more than a superficial glance.

"People will never see all there is to see in a picture," notes Marvin Heiferman (2012), author of *Photography Changes Everything*. "Because we are wired to start looking for one specific thing when we come upon an image, it's virtually guaranteed that we will fail to notice much of the other content that is embedded in it."

Heiferman is alluding to research that indicates people tend to quickly categorize images instead of looking at them. They think: *It's a race car . . . ugh, I really hate NASCAR.* Or: *Hey, it's a puppy! So cute! I love dogs!* Human brains have evolved the ability to quickly sort and categorize images. So how can we help students become smarter at "reading" the images they see?

The Learning Network at the *New York Times* has attempted to address this problem with a popular feature titled, "What's Going On in This Picture?" This section is operated by Visual Learning Strategies (VTS), an educational group that helps teachers enhance the visual literacy of their students. "What's Going On in This Picture" runs every Monday in the *New York Times*. They provide an intriguing photo along with three questions for students to consider:

What's going on in this picture?

What do you see that makes you say that?

What more can you find?

Yoon Kang-O'Higgins is senior trainer at VTS. I asked her why it's important for kids to be able to look critically at a photograph.

"We live in such a visual world," Yoon replied. "We are inundated with images, but we can't take these images at face value. If we can't think critically about those images, we're lost. The first line of making meaning is unpacking that image."

Yoon also mentioned people's tendency to give photographs no more than a cursory glance. "In museums people spend an average of eight to eleven seconds in front of an image. We want students to look at one image for fifteen minutes."

The approach suggested by VTS relies heavily on conversation, especially peer-to-peer talk. Kids are encouraged to discuss the photo with other students in class. Yoon talked about the important of creating a "sticky moment," a concept derived from what VTS has learned from watching curators lead art tours in museums.

"Our research shows that even when curators were giving vibrant talks about art, not much of it sticks to the listeners because the talk was too high level," Yoon said. "A conversation will be 'stickier' when kids are having a conversation with other peers, when everybody is speaking at roughly the same level."

In addition to fostering classroom discussion about an image, the "What's Going On in This Picture?" feature also provides a format for students to chat (via blogs) with students in other places.

"Students tend to be locked into their own community and school," Yoon said. "Our online discussion brings students together from various areas of the country and around the world. Kids become more sophisticated in their comments, demonstrating deeper analysis, after being exposed to other students in other communities."

THE PHOTOGRAPH AS MENTOR TEXT

Can a photograph be considered a "mentor text"? Yes. Like a poem or essay, a photo provides an example or model from which we can all learn. However, there are certainly differences between texts and images. Texts contain letters assembled to build words that are combined to create sentences, and so forth. Unlike most writing, photos contain color, shapes, and visual objects. But there are many similarities as well. Like a piece of writing, a photograph does all of the following:

- represents a form of communication
- facilitates self-expression
- is an abstraction (and not the real thing)
- exists in two dimensions
- can provoke a range of emotions
- involves the viewer in a cognitive process
- invites multiple rereadings/reviewings
- is transactional (i.e., it invites each reader to make his or her own meaning, one that may be different from the meaning made by someone else).

Adam Myman and Janelle Barker coteach a fourth-grade class in North Hills, California. In the past few years they have been devising ways to help their students become smarter at interpreting photographs. They begin by sharing a variety of images with their students. These photos become an integral part of the language arts curriculum; they also feature prominently in science and social studies. I asked Adam how they decide which photos to use.

"We try to choose a photo that will spark a great conversation," Adam told me. "To choose a photo, you really have to know your kids. Are they sports junkies? Then start with a sports photo. I'm always thinking about the kid who is at the fringe of things. How do I get *that* kid involved?"

Adam went to a workshop showing how you can divide a painting into sections and have students talk about each section. That gave him an idea. Adam has always been passionate about rock music.

"I was shocked to realize that there's a whole generation of kids who don't know anything about album covers," he said. "When I was young, we considered album covers true works of art."

He and Janelle wanted to select an album cover for their kids to study. They chose *Abbey Road* by The Beatles. They looked at the cover, wondering: What kinds of things could they get the students talking about?

They divided the cover into four quadrants of equal size. Each day they uncovered a different section and asked their students to look closely at it. To get them started, Adam and Janelle suggested language to get students thinking and talking about the image:

I think . . .

I wonder . . .

I bet . . . (making predictions)

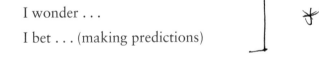

In addition, Adam and Janelle asked a series of questions:

What did you notice about the setting?

What did you notice about the characters?

Did you have an emotional reaction or connection to this picture?

They found it helpful to provide structure for these discussions, at least at first. They asked students to do the following:

◆ Turn and share.

◆ Stop and jot.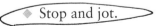

◆ Hand over their journal to the person next to them.

◆ Read the partner's entry and discuss.

This led to a whole-class discussion that lasted roughly fifteen minutes. These sessions took place on four consecutive days, in the same week.

"For a culminating activity," Adam told me, "we listened to the songs on the album."

Adam and Janelle wanted their students to do a "close reading" of one photograph, and they used Adam's passion for rock music as a starting point. They made time and space for their students to talk and think their way into the images. Like the educators at VTS, Adam and Janelle believe that talk is a crucial part of meaning making.

"Our school embraces a talking curriculum," Adam says. "That's when the big observations and connections happen—when kids are talking."

I encourage teachers to take the plunge and invite students to study images. Don't feel like you must have it all figured out; you can learn alongside your students. Have fun with it. Encourage students to talk whenever possible, and don't be surprised if there are some awkward silences. Feel free to use any image from this book, from a magazine, or from the "What's Going On in This Picture?" feature in the *New York Times*. I also recommend "Every Photo Is a Story," a video series created by the Library of Congress.

One provocative image—that's all you really need. I love the photos of Bill Owens. Take a look at *Suburbia* (1999), images that portray Californians in the 1970s. One picture shows a harried housewife holding a baby in a kitchen.

Invite your students to look closely at this picture. You might toss out a few questions to get the discussion rolling:

- What details do you notice?

- What does her facial expression tell you?

- From looking at her hairstyle, when do you think this photo was taken?

- Why did the photographer pull back to include the dirty dishes?

- How would the photo have been different if the dishes were not included?

Bill Owens, **Suburbia**

QUESTIONS FOR HELPING STUDENTS UNPACK A PHOTOGRAPH

What's going on in this picture?

What do you see that makes you say that?

What do you see in the foreground? The background?

Who is present/represented in this picture?

Who is absent from this picture?

What feeling do you get while viewing this photo?

What more can you find?

Where are your eyes drawn first? Later?

Do you see yourself in this photograph? If so, where?

Is there any life lesson in this photo?

Photographing
to Learn

Once upon a time, educators viewed writing as a way for students to demonstrate what they knew. In other words, it gave us a way to check up on them. Kids wrote to regurgitate what they had learned. This attitude toward writing persisted for a long time until William Zinsser, James Moffett, Don Murray, and a few others put forth a different view. They argued that rather than being a passive activity, writing is an active way to learn—uncover tacit knowledge, make connections, synthesize, tease out nagging questions. Today, most best practice writing instruction embraces this more enlightened view.

A similar principle applies to photography. You might imagine photography simply as a way to capture/record what you see. It can certainly function like that, but it turns out that photography is also a powerful tool for learning. Snapping pictures has allowed me to take a crash course on the natural world. I have learned a ton about tides, reflection, animal anatomy, courtship, mating, predation, feeding the young. . . . For instance, while taking photographs I noticed the following:

◆ The merganser has a serrated bill (form), a feature that's extremely useful for grasping and holding slippery fish (function).

◆ A cormorant's neck can expand (form) when swallowing a fish (function).

Eastern Phoebe with Chick

◆ The ruby-throated hummingbird is territorial and will chase away another hummer that wants to approach the feeder. There's only one exception: I've noticed that during a steady rain some hummingbirds will reluctantly allow other hummers to come to the feeder and drink. It's comical to see two or three tiny, wet birds perched on the feeder, a temporary truce between them.

At times one of my images reveals something unexpected. One morning I set up my camera to photograph a nest of phoebe chicks situated above our front door. Phoebes are flycatchers; the parents ferry an astonishing assortment of live insects to their hungry chicks. I noticed that one chick seemed to be monopolizing the parents' attention, gobbling down nearly all the food. My wife and I dubbed that chick "Baby Huey" because it of its comically large size. We were struck by the palpable bond between the baby bird and the parents.

I continued photographing the phoebes. One day, when reviewing my photos, I was startled to see this one:

One blurry photo changed everything.

Wait—what? It's not a sharp picture, but underneath Baby Huey I could make out two distinct shapes with beaks. Those shapes looked an awful lot like smaller chicks. This image confused and rattled me and threw my understanding of phoebes into question. Had the phoebe female laid a successive brood—eggs that would hatch a few weeks apart? I'd never heard of such a thing. And yet the evidence was right in front of me.

When I did some research, I uncovered a startling fact. The Eastern phoebe is commonly parasitized by the cowbird. Instead of building a nest of its own, the cowbird lays eggs in the nests of other birds. Phoebes are frequent victims. This presents a serious danger to phoebes, whose blood offspring often get malnourished and don't survive. So the large chick was a cowbird! I can report that my story has a happy ending: one day later Baby Huey left the nest. The phoebe parents continued to feed the other babies, who gained weight and eventually fledged. Whew!

This may sound like a rather extreme anecdote, but it has happened to me many times. And I'm not unique in this regard. This cycle involving photographic discovery happens every day, in many fields of knowledge, all over the world:

We start with a certain understanding of the world.

We take detailed, close-up photographs.

We study those images.

Those pictures reveal something surprising/unexpected that challenges our worldview.

This sparks a series of new questions.

This leads to further investigation (and often the need for additional photographs).

We revise our thinking and end up with a new, more accurate understanding of the world. It's worth noting that my new learning was prompted not by a sharp image, but a weak, out-of-focus shot.

A photographer recently posted a remarkable image of a female merganser followed by a line of seventy-six chicks. This picture prompted a good deal of head-scratching: could all the chicks possibly be from the same mother, perhaps part of some super brood? An intense discussion ensued; ornithologists weighed in from near and far. It turns out that some birds (including mergansers) raise their babies using a childcare system known as a crèche—mothers leave their babies in the care of an older female who is experienced at raising babies (Mervosh 2018).

Observation plays a crucial role in this dynamic. Taking pictures forces you to pay close attention to your subject—you can't help it. I observe closely during various stages of the photographic process:

- Watching the subject ahead of time. Careful observation helps me predict where my subject is likely to move next. That way I can be one step ahead of the bird (or toddler).

- Taking the actual picture. At that moment the rest of the world disappears; my attention is laser-focused on the subject at hand.

- Reviewing the photos later and, perhaps, discovering something that surprises me.

We know that observation—paying close attention to what you see—helps students learn about the world. Taking photos might help students hone their powers of observation. But what kind of photos should be used? Typically, kids look at photographs from books, newspapers, magazines, websites, or other sources. I asked a number of teachers if they ever use photographs kids have taken themselves in the classroom? Nearly every teacher offered the same response: "No, but that's an intriguing idea."

I suggest we get students taking their own photos, either with their smartphones, iPads, or inexpensive digital cameras. Encouraging students to take their own photographs would seem to have at least two benefits:

1. It will make them less passive/more engaged.
2. It will sharpen their powers of observation.

So far, so good. But it turns out that there's a fly in the soup, a serious one that should give us pause. Psychologist Linda Henkel (2013) has studied the impact of photography on memory. Henkel asked the question: does taking a photo of something help you remember it better? She conducted an experiment with a group of students at a museum. The first group observed art for thirty seconds. The second group observed art for twenty seconds and then photographed it. The following day both groups answered questions about the art they had seen at the museum.

Henkel discovered that the students who had photographed the artwork remembered *fewer* objects and *fewer* details than the kids who observed the art without photographing it. She dubbed this the "photo-taking-impairment effect."

This is sobering. Henkel's data suggest that asking kids to take photos can make students more passive and less engaged. I resisted this idea at first, but the more I thought about it the more I realized that Henkel has hit on an uncomfortable truth. It's quite possible to snap a picture of something without really observing it, maybe telling yourself: "Well, I have the picture, so I can look at it later." Often you never do.

At a later date, Henkel repeated her students-at-the-museum study with one important change. This time, she asked kids who took the photos to zoom in on one part of the image. She discovered that zooming in reversed the photo-taking-impairment effect. Those students did a much better job remembering what they had seen.

"It may be that our photos can help us remember only if we actually access and interact with them, rather than just amass them," Henkel concluded.

Photography can certainly be a powerful learning tool, but it's not just a matter of setting kids loose with their smartphones or iPads and saying: "Go to it!" It will be important to lean in and structure this experience for students so they don't merely collect photos but continue to interact with them. An activity involving student-generated photos might look something like this:

- ◆ Give direction on how to photograph.

- ◆ Suggest kids come up with a focus. You could suggest one (photograph the subject's hands) or have students devise their own focus.

- ◆ Make time for kids to review their images. They can ask themselves:

  - ❖ What do I notice?

  - ❖ Did I see anything unexpected?

  - ❖ Did I learn anything new?

- ◆ Encourage students to sort, categorize, tag, or label their images.

- ◆ Schedule time for students to dialogue with each other and report out their findings.

The concept of learning-through-photography makes me think of *Blow-Up*, an Italian movie directed by Michelangelo Antonioni. In this film a man takes photos at a park. Later, while developing those images in the dark room, he's horrified to realize that he has accidentally photographed a murder. This is a reminder that we can never discount the impact of chance and dumb luck.

Much of what I learn while taking photos has been unplanned. Photography is a powerful tool for inquiry. Taking pictures and studying them can lead to a deeper understanding the world, but they aren't foolproof. Or maybe it's more accurate to say that we are not foolproof. Humans have a remarkable ability to deceive ourselves. Sometimes we refuse to see what the photo is telling us.

My mother had nine kids. She had a remarkable ability to juggle the demands of our huge household: shopping, cooking, cleaning, paying bills, attending to kids' schedules, and so on. My mother's life didn't become calmer until the last Fletcher finally moved out of the house. Finally, she could read, travel, and enjoy a leisurely lunch with a friend.

One Christmas, when my mother was sixty-six, she bought sweaters for the gals in our family but mixed up the sizes. That wasn't like her. During the next six months she forgot several birthdays. One day she got lost while driving home from the supermarket. She insisted she was fine, but my father finally persuaded her to go see a specialist. Tests revealed that my mother had undergone serious memory loss. Her condition worsened steadily. After she died, at the age of seventy-four, an autopsy confirmed that she had Alzheimer's.

Let's rewind the tape. By the time my mother was seventy, we all knew for certain she had full-blown dementia. But when I look at photographs of my mother taken a few years earlier, when she was sixty-six or sixty-seven, I recognize a confused expression in her eyes, the look of someone profoundly lost. Photographs don't lie. Those pictures reveal to me that my mother was probably suffering from dementia years before I realized it. The evidence was right in front of me, but I couldn't—or wouldn't—see it.

Valerie Bang-Jensen and Mark Lubkowitz (2017) are the authors of *Sharing Books, Talking Science*. Here they share a few thoughts on how photography can enrich the classroom.

- Photos are an excellent tool for identifying or discovering the crosscutting concepts, precisely because they freeze a moment in time. A photo captures a hovering hummingbird, allowing us to visualize the motion (energy!) of the wings, something we cannot see with the naked eye.

- Like illustrations, photographs allow us to see scientific concepts but with much more accuracy. We can actually see pollen on a bee's knees, which invites us to think about structure and function.

- A lightning bolt in a photograph whispers to us that something is about to happen, suggesting cause and effect and energy transformation.

- Have your students take photos to discover and document the crosscutting concepts in action, like a classmate running (energy), a dandelion seed being carried by the wind (structure and function), or ripples forming in a puddle (cause and effect).

How Photographs
Spark Writing
(or Do They?)

D on't force it.

Your students' photographs can certainly act as springboards for their writing, but don't force this connection. As much as possible, allow the link between their photos and their writing to evolve naturally.

Invite? Yes.

Demonstrate? Definitely.

Assign? Sparingly. By their very nature, assignments limit choice (even if it's only the choice of whether or not to complete the assignment). When you give an assignment, you start drawing down a bank account of student engagement, one with finite funds. When it comes to writing from photographs, why not find out what students are already doing in this regard, go with their energy, and see if we might redirect their flow? In this chapter we'll look at authentic ways student photos can lead them to do more writing. I'm drawing on teachers I know and their classrooms, but I'm also drawing on my own experience. I began by asking myself: when/how do the pictures I take lead me to write?

Incoming!

Beak Duel

Red-Naped Sapsucker on Sap Well

Writing a caption. Taking a picture is one thing; sharing it is another. When I email a picture to a friend or relative ("Email is so yesterday, Dad!"), I almost always add a comment or caption. It seems abrupt or even rude to send a photo without some written remark. Sometimes I provide a simple label or brief description. Often, I can't resist making an editorial comment.

"I'm an open book: I've got nothing to hide!"

Although the label on the picture of the sapsucker is accurate, it doesn't explain very much. An effective caption can also provide important context or further information, extending the information already provided by the image: "The red-naped sapsucker creates a sap well by peeling away the bark. Sapsuckers know that removing all the bark will kill the tree; they leave enough bark so the sap can still flow up and down the trunk."

If you scroll through your Facebook or Instagram feed, you'll be struck by how many photos are accompanied by captions that are funny, playful, often irreverent. One way of creating humor is to devise a caption as voice-over, giving the photographic subject an imagined line of dialogue. I did so with the above photo of a cormorant drying its wings.

When my colleague Dan Feigelson confers with younger readers, he often issues an invitation: "Can you say more about that?" In a similar way, a caption is an invitation to *say more about* an image and to put your personal stamp on it. The fact that captions are short and pithy (often no more than a word or two) makes this a nonthreatening microgenre for young writers.

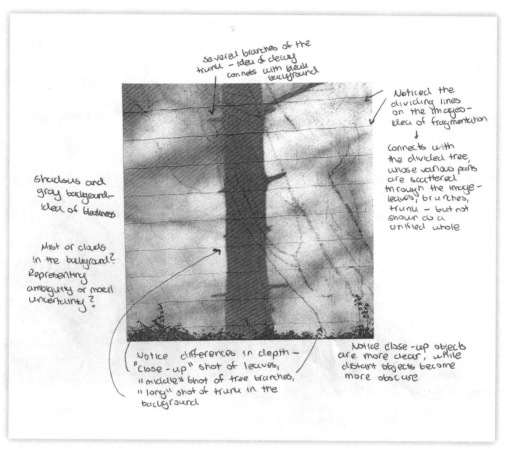

Annotating a Photograph

Annotating an image. Tim Reisert, who teaches at an all-male high school in Ohio, wanted his students to delve deeper into visual images. He invites them to write comments and observations in the white spaces around an image, as we can see here.

"I find if my students can annotate images they can eventually translate those skills to annotating written texts," Reisert says.

*Creating a meme. The meme is a grassroots genre that sprung up organically and carved out a place in the world. Memes consist of humorous photos or video clips, usually accompanied by text. They are copied, often altered, and usually spread via social media.

Like any persuasive essay, memes can shape our thinking about political, social, and personal issues. There's a built-in audience. Whoever constructs a meme knows their creation is likely to elicit feedback, which is a huge motivator. No wonder kids love making them.

I'm having a very bad day.

Writing from a photo. I was standing in a clearing when a pileated wood-pecker suddenly landed on a nearby tree, accompanied by a loud, raucous cry. I was thrilled. With its huge size and spectacular plumage, the pileated woodpecker is a rock star in the bird world. I grabbed a few pictures before the bird left.

Later, after I had downloaded the photos onto my computer, I had time to study this one. As I did so, I could almost feel the language part of my brain engage and slowly start to turn. Words began trickling into my brain, so I took out my notebook and started to write.

Pileated Woodpecker

Pileated
woodpecker
keeps its food
locked
in tall
swaying
cabinets
and never
has to worry
about losing
the key.

I printed the photo and the poem, and arranged them side by side in my writer's notebook. The image was a catalyst for the poem. You might counter: but wasn't it the bird rather than the image that inspired the poem? Actually,

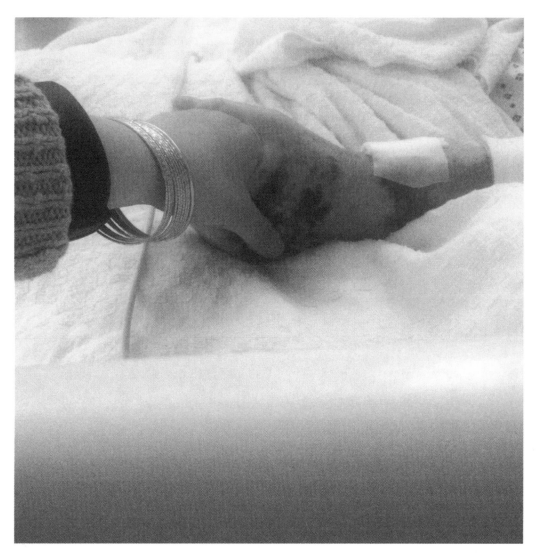

A daughter bids farewell to her father.

no. In the heat of the moment, when the bird flies in, I'm all business, trying to get the photo. Later, when I'm looking at the images, I find myself in a more reflective mood. That's when I feel like writing.

Jen Greene, second-grade teacher, told me a poignant story involving an important photograph.

"My father battled brain cancer for seven years before passing away in late 2016. This is a picture that I snapped quickly when he reached for my hand the last time he was in the hospital. While he did not have the words, he knew I needed him. It was a moment I wanted to remember, and while neither of us could speak, the picture captured all the emotion that failed me in words."

Jen says: "Later, after I was able to process the permanency of what was happening, I used that photograph to write this poem, which might not have come to be if I hadn't thought to preserve that moment."

My heartbeat sped up
When yours slowed down
Like two freight trains
Headed in opposite directions
I gripped your hand
As if I could transfer
Energy
To bring you back
It's amazing that my heart can still beat
Even after being shattered
into pieces

Jen's Poem

To summarize, these are the key ideas in this chapter:

◆ Don't force the links between photos and writing.

◆ Tap into real-world genres (e.g., the meme) that are familiar to students.

◆ Encourage students to write from photos they have taken themselves.

◆ Don't expect students to immediately write from a picture they have taken. Allow a cushion of time, a pause, so they can sit with the photo awhile.

During a recent trip to British Columbia I had the chance to photograph loons on a small lake near Kamloops. This picture captures one bird at first light.

Later that evening I sorted through all my pictures, discarding the clunkers, trying to identify the keepers. The image on page 101 was one of my favorites, and later it prompted me to write a haiku:

ruby-eyed beauty
swimming through dappled shadow
takes my breath away

I sent this image and the accompanying poem to my longtime friend Mike McCormick. He is a naturalist, writer, and former fifth-grade teacher.

Loon in the Reeds

"It's one of your best photos: almost breathtakingly intimate," he wrote back. "But the photo doesn't need the haiku. The haiku couldn't successfully stand alone without the photo. Paired with the photo, the haiku detracts from the picture."

Well, *that's* pretty harsh, I thought. I sulked for a few hours. But later, after letting this response sink in, it dawned on me that Mike was probably right. And he wasn't being mean. He was simply trying to be direct and forthright— we have that kind of friendship. That day I learned an important lesson. A photograph can certainly act as catalyst for writing, but words don't always enhance a picture. Sometimes a photograph needs to breathe, to be surrounded by nothing but space and silence, to stand on its own.

Double Exposure:
Ralph Talks to Ralph

Q: Do you believe visual images (including photographs) represent another way of thinking? Or are they extensions of traditional literacy?

A: That's the question. You can make an argument both ways. I honestly don't know. The jury is still out. I suspect photographs do represent another way—a wordless, nontextual way—for people to understand the world, interact with it, and express our truths. It's certainly a powerful mode of communication. We know that Florence has struck North Carolina because we see a picture of the swirling cloud on a TV screen across the room. Words aren't always necessary. Remember: cognitive scientists tell us that human brains are wired for processing images.

I certainly don't think we need to choose sides: text or image. I think it's possible for the visual and the textual to peacefully coexist, for one to enhance the other. That's the view I put forth in this book.

Q: Do you believe photography can enrich the writing workshop?

A: For sure. Like any photographer, a writer is an image maker. We describe carefully because we want the reader to see the world we're creating in our text.

But it's not just photography—it's also the language of photography. Writing teachers talk to students about *show, don't tell* or *exploding a moment.* Labels like that represent a kind of verbal shorthand. They certainly have a place in the classroom, but after a while these slogans grow stale. The world of photography gives teachers a different way to talk about writing using a fresh new language. That's how I came up with the title of this book: *Focus Lessons.* While learning to take pictures, I've been struck by how many terms apply as much to writing as they do photography. It's uncanny.

Q: It sounds like you're encouraging literacy teachers to embrace photography. Does this require a shift in thinking?

A: I do think we need to think differently. When we observe a boy taking pictures, we may tend to think: *He's fooling around with his cell phone.* What if we thought instead: *He's composing. He's constructing an argument, thinking hard about how best to persuade his viewers. He's creating a story.*

Q: In recent years programs like Photoshop and Lightroom have become very popular. Is postprocessing in photography akin to revision in writing?

A: I think postprocessing is more akin to editing. Most people use those programs to change the surface features of the image (contrast, color) rather than to alter the substance/content.

Q: Do photographers revise? If so, how?

A: Don Murray often said: "Write early, and write fast." That's another piece of advice that applies to taking pictures. One advantage of photography is that you can work fast. You can try different "drafts" of an image by using a lower angle or experimenting with a slower shutter speed. And you can take those pictures in rapid succession. So, in that sense, yes, photographers are constantly revising their work. I know I am.

Q: Do you spend a lot of time postprocessing your images?

A: Sometimes. Postprocessing programs certainly make it easy to tweak a photo. You can cut down the glare here, make the colors pop there. You can improve an image during postprocessing . . . but only to a point.

I find that my best images jump out at me. I see a certain picture in the camera's viewfinder and say: "Oh!" I know right away that it's a good one. A really strong image doesn't need a lot of postprocessing.

Don't get lazy and expect to rescue a weak image by doctoring it up with Lightroom or some other program. Get it right the first time. That's my mantra. If it doesn't look right, if it's not what I want, I make some adjustments (shooting angle, shutter speed, etc.) in the field and try more shots.

Q: You emphasize the importance of students taking their own photographs. Can you say more about that?

A: Just to be clear, I don't think we should rely *only* on photographs kids have taken themselves. I think there's value for students (as well as teachers) to study powerful images taken by great photographers and consider: what makes this image work? We can all learn from the masters (Chapter 6).

But I hope teachers will also encourage students to take their own photographs. Kids are already taking tons of pictures on their own, so it's a matter of sanctioning this activity and bringing it into the classroom. Photographing is a way of composing. Most teachers would agree that students should be doing the writing—not us—so it would make sense to use images that students took themselves. It will be much more meaningful and engaging to use their own pictures. That way we can harness their passions. And they can think hard about all the decisions that went into creating those images.

Q: In Chapter 3, you talk about how you increasingly find yourself using your camera as your writer's notebook.

A: Yes. That's one of the big ideas in this book.

Q: Do you think that's true for our students? Are they using their smartphone cameras in the same way we want them to use a notebook for writing?

A: Not exactly the same way, but pretty close. I think we may need to reimagine what we mean by the writer's notebook. It doesn't have to be limited to sentences and paragraphs scribbled on blank paper. It could also be a blizzard of images—photos, flash video, drawings, and cartoons. When we look at this kind of notebook we may ask: OK, fine, but where's the writing? In some cases, the writing gets added when the photo gets shared with a friend or on social media. In other cases, as I've said, the image stands alone. That has to be OK.

I asked several educators to comment on the idea of smartphone camera as writer's notebook.

"Notebooking is so natural with smartphones and photos," said Franki Sibberson, coauthor of *Digital Reading: What's Essential in Grades 3–8* (2015). "Kids are living their lives as writers and storytellers in the ways we worked at so hard to accomplish before this technology was available. *We worked so hard to provide authentic audiences, and now kids have them. So much of what we hoped for is right in their phone*" (my italics).

Darren Victory, a fourth-grade teacher in Texas, had an interesting perspective: "I think the phone is more comparable to a bookshelf that holds several writer's notebooks, each with its own purpose. Facebook, Snapchat, personal photo files, Instagram, images we send via text or email to a specific person . . . all these conversations are logged in specific places depending on purpose and audience. The cell phone is simply another way to 'shelve' our many notebooks."

Q: Has your sojourn into serious photography followed a particular sequence?

A: My learning is ongoing—I'm definitely not "there" yet—and it has been anything but sequential. It continues to be simultaneous . . . happening at once. I feel like I'm still on the steep end of the learning curve. The more you know, the more you know how much you don't know.

For example, in "Bring Something Strong" (page 44), I mentioned the photo of a pigeon guillemot coming in with its "landing gear" deployed. I was surprised to discover that people liked this grainy image. I discovered that viewers tended to focus on the red feet and were willing to overlook the other flaws. I didn't expect that. I suspect this is true in writing, as well. How many otherwise forgettable poems and books get lodged in our memory because of one arresting line or image? Once we get grabbed, we stay grabbed.

I believe in the past few years schools have promoted a kind of bland writing—competent but lifeless. (I explore this idea in depth in *Joy Write* [2017].) It may fulfill the basic requirements, but does it grab the reader? I would say no. And that's unfortunate. Maybe student writing needs more bright red feet!

Q: Do literacy teachers tend to give a cold shoulder to photos and other visuals?

A: Some do. And frankly there was a time when I would have included myself in that group. By training and by nature, literacy teachers are language lovers. We savor powerful metaphors and beautiful writing. Sometimes our hackles go up if we catch kids doodling or drawing during class. "You're wasting time. You should be writing!"

Interesting that we equate creating an image to wasting time! In the meantime, the world keeps turning. Our culture evolves. The visual world keeps banging on the classroom door.

"Let me in!"

"We're writing essays!" we yell. "We're reading Shelley and Keats! Go away!"

But the visual world won't go away. It's here to stay. I encourage literacy teachers to make a move that may feel counterintuitive at first. Open the door and invite photographs into the room. Make a place for them at the table. Your students already know more about this world than you might think. And, as I've said, you don't have to have it all figured out. You can learn with your students, side by side.

Q: What practical steps or activities could teachers do to bring photography into the classroom?

A: I would encourage teachers to take a look at the Self-E Expression Project (see Appendix D for more information). Here's a chance to tap into a genre (the selfie) that kids know well. Have students go on a treasure hunt (either inside or outside) to photograph the alphabet. This is a fun, nonthreatening way to sharpen their observation skills while they start playing with photography.

Q: Final question. What made you shed your persona as a writer and become photographer?

A: Whoa, slow down. I haven't shed anything. At my core I'm still a writer. That's how I will always define myself.

Q: OK. So, what's the source of your passion for photography?

A: Hmm. Well, a couple of things. First, taking pictures has allowed me to see and savor—and collect—the rampant beauty of this world. I've discovered beauty in the tiniest things—a dewdrop on a spider web skewered by a ray of morning sun. To see something beautiful like that—wow! It feels like being brushed by an angel's wings. And then to be able to capture such loveliness, even imperfectly, is a marvelous thing.

Second, taking pictures has deepened my understanding and appreciation of the natural world. I have learned the names of hundreds of bird species, as well as plants, trees, and insects. My vocabulary in that realm has expanded greatly.

Finally, photography has taught me how to live in the present moment. We all know the slogans: *be here now, live in the present, all we have is now*. Easier said than done. We are forever fretting about the past and the future: Why did I say that to him? How can I lose these twenty pounds? Will my son get accepted to college? Will I get tenure?

Photography has taught me how to tune out (most of) those worrisome voices. A photograph is a record of a single moment in time. The "metadata" of a photo records the precise moment it was taken. Taking pictures forces me to climb out of myself, to shut off my ego. At the moment I squeeze the shutter, I'm totally focused (in both senses of the word) on my subject. I'm breathing the oxygen of the moment. I'm stapled to the now. That's where I want to live.

The End

[O] APPENDIX A

Resources for Finding Photographs

What's Going On in This Picture?

The New York Times
www.nytimes.com/column/learning-whats-going-on-in-this-picture

Every Photo Is a Story

The Library of Congress
www.loc.gov/rr/print/coll/fbj/Every_Photo_home.html

These websites a wide range of free images that are appropriate for the classroom:

Photos for Class . . . . www.photosforclass.com

Flicker Commons . . . . . . www.flickr.com/commons

Pics4Learning www.Pics4Learning.com

Pixabay . . . . https://pixabay.com

Pexels . . . . www.pexels.com

Kaboompics . . . . https://kaboompics.com/gallery

Unsplash . . . . https://unsplash.com

Gratisography . . . . https://gratisography.com

Negative Space . . . . https://negativespace.co

[O] APPENDIX B

Photographers and Their Websites (a partial list)

Glenn Bartley . . . . www.glennbartley.com

Greg Basco . . . . www.deepgreenphotography.com

Spencer Cox . . . . www.spencercoxphoto.com

Joshua Cripps . . . . www.joshuacripps.com

Greg Downing. . . . . www.naturescapes.net

Wendy Ewald . . . . www.wendyewald.com

Denise Ippolito . . . . www.deniseippolito.com

Adam Jones. . . . . www.adamjonesphoto.com

Anne McKinnell . . . . www.annemckinnell.com

Arthur Morris . . . . www.birdsasart.com

Alan Murphy . . . . www.alanmurphyphotography.com

Bill Owens. . . . . www.billowens.com

Sarah Skinner . . . . www.imagesofwildlife.co.uk

Destin Sparks . . . . www.destinsparks.com

Guy Tal . . . . https://guytal.com

David H. Wells . . . . www.davidhwells.com

[O] APPENDIX C

Wendy Ewald, Photographer
http://wendyewald.com

Wendy Ewald's work is directed toward helping children see and using the camera as a tool for expression. In 1989 she created the "Literacy Through Photography" programs in Durham, North Carolina, and Houston, Texas. She is currently working on a project with schools in Tanzania. Her bold school-based projects often delve into issues of identity, underrepresentation, and social justice. See for example:

Black Self/White Self

 http://wendyewald.com/portfolio/black-self-white-self

Wendy Ewald books include:

American Alphabets. 2005. New York: Scalo. Ewald says: "I use the alphabet to break down a big subject in a playful way . . . refugees and immigrants, for example."

 The Best Part of Me: Children Talk About Their Bodies in Pictures and Words. 2002. New York: Little Brown.

I Wanna Take Me a Picture: Teaching Photography and Writing to Children. 2001. Boston; Beacon Press.

 Literacy and Justice Through Photography: A Classroom Guide. With Katherine Hynde and Lisa Lord. 2011. New York: Teachers College Press.

[◎] APPENDIX D

The Self-E Expression Project with Joan McGarry

[handwritten margin note: Grade 5, Unit 1?]

Joan McGarry is Director of Education and Visitor Engagement at the Westmoreland Museum of American Art in Greensburg, Pennsylvania. She had created the Self-E Expression Project where students take selfies and then write about the images using these questions as guidelines.

Selfie/Self-E

(Self-Explanation) At face value/on the surface—Just the facts

- What are my physical characteristics? (Color of my hair, eyes. Shape of face. Describe features in as much detail as possible.)
- What age am I? (Can this be guessed from my portrait?)
- What does the way I am posing say about me?
- What does my facial expression say?

(Self-Exploration) Going a little deeper—Fleshing myself out

- What do my clothes, hair, makeup, jewelry, say about me? (This also falls under self-explanation and self-expression.)
- What groups do I belong to (family, friends, school, after school, community, etc.)?
- What are my interests/hobbies?
- What is my heritage? Do I identify with a particular cultural group? Are there traditions or rituals that I participate in?
- What are some of the things that are important to me (objects, people, places)?

(Self-Expression) Below the surface—A deeper understanding of who I am

- How have the above things shaped and defined me?
- How can I express these things that make me me: my personality, my emotions, my beliefs, my thoughts, my feelings, my creative/expressive self? In words and in images.

(Self-Endorsement) I am the sum of all my parts. I am more than my face and physical appearance. I have value. I matter.

How do I distill all of the above into one image that expresses and validates me?

⦿ WORKS CITED

Bang-Jensen, Valerie, and Mark Lubkowitz. 2017. *Sharing Books, Talking Science: Exploring Scientific Concepts with Children's Literature*. Portsmouth, NH: Heinemann.

Bryan, Trevor. 2019. *The Art of Comprehension: Exploring Visual Texts to Foster Comprehension, Conversation, and Confidence*. Portsmouth, NH: Stenhouse.

Cox, Spencer. 2018. "How Light Creates Emotion in Photography." https://photographylife.com/landscapes/how-light-creates-emotion-in-photography.

Cripps, Joshua. 2016. "Better Composition: Use Leading Lines to Improve Your Photos." www.joshuacripps.com/2016/03/better-composition-use-leading-lines-improve-photos/.

Eiseley, Loren. 1959. *The Immense Journey: An Imaginative Naturalist Explores the Myteries of Man and Nature*. New York: Vintage.

Every Photo Is a Story. www.loc.gov/rr/print/coll/fbj/Every_Photo_home.html. Washington, DC: The Library of Congress.

Fletcher, Ralph. 1997. *Spider Boy*. New York: Houghton Mifflin Sandpiper.

———. 2007. *The One O'Clock Chop*. New York: Henry Holt & Co.

———. 2015. *Marshfield Dreams: When I Was a Kid*. New York: Henry Holt Books for Children.

———. 2017. *Joy Write: Cultivating High-Impact, Low-Stakes Writing*. Portsmouth, NH: Heinemann.

———. 2018. *Marshfield Memories: More Stories About Growing Up*. New York: Henry Holt Books for Children.

Fletcher, Ralph, and JoAnn Portalupi. 2007. *Craft Lessons: Teaching Writing K–8*. Portsmouth, NH: Stenhouse.

Harvey, Stephanie, and Annie Ward. 2017. *From Striving to Thriving: How to Grow Confident, Capable Readers*. New York: Scholastic.

Heiferman, Marvin. 2012. *Photography Changes Everything*. New York: Aperture.

Henkel, Linda A. December. 2013. "Point-and-Shoot Memories: The Influence of Taking Photos on Memory for a Museum Tour." www.researchgate.net/publication/259207719_PointandShoot_Memories_The_Influence_of_Taking_Photos_on_Memory_for_a_Museum_Tour.

Janeczko, Paul. 2007. *Worlds Afire*. Boston: Candlewick.

Mervosh, Sarah. 2018. "1 Hen, 76 Ducklings: What's the Deal with This Picture?" *New York Times*, July 24. www.nytimes.com/2018/07/24/science/merganser-ducklings-photo.html.

Murray, Donald. 1989. *Expecting the Unexpected: Teaching Myself and Others to Read and Write*. Portsmouth, NH: Heinemann.

———. 2001. *My Twice-Lived Life: A Memoir*. New York: Ballantine Books.

Nep, Casey N. 2014. "A Thousand Words: Writing from Photographs." *The New Yorker Magazine*, February 26.

Newkirk, Thomas. 2017. *Embarrassment: And the Emotional Underlife of Learning*. Portsmouth, NH: Heinemann.

Owens, Bill. *Suburbia*. 1999. New York: Fotofolio.

Pritchett, David. 2019. "How to Capture Mood In Your Photos." www.ephotozine.com /article/how-to-capture-mood-in-your-photos-27246

Sibberson, Franki. 2015. *Digital Reading: What's Essential in Grades 3–8*. Urbana, IL: NCTE.

Smith, Laura. 2016. "Are Photographs a Truly Reliable Primary Source?" UCONN. University Libraries Archives and Special Collections Blog. https://blogs.lib.uconn.edu /archives/2016/07/29/are-photographs-a-truly-reliable-primary-source/.

Tal, Guy. 2018. "Create Visual Tension." *Outdoor Photographer*, November 6. www .outdoorphotographer.com/tips-techniques/nature-landscapes/create-visual-tension.

Time. "Top 10 Doctored Photos." http://content.time.com/time/photogallery/0,29307 ,1924226,00.html.